What Women Need to Know About Male Sexual Addiction

(Third Edition.)

MaryLou Swanberg, MA, FCC,BT
Paul Becker, MAEd, LPC

1

First publisher: AuthorHouse under the title: Why Is My Partner Sexually Addicted? Insight Women Need 02/14/2012

Second publisher: Createspace under the title: What Women Need to Know about Male Sexual Addiction 02/15/2016

Third publisher: Createspace under the title: What Women Need to Know about Male Sexual Addiction 06/30/2019 (Third Edition)

Updated version of: *Why Is My Partner Sexually Addicted?*

ISBN: 13 — 978-107618385

ISBN: 10 – 152337893x

Printed in the United States of America

Books Authored by Paul Becker, LPC

(732) 224-2020
One Step

Letters from Paul

In Search of Recovery: A Christian Man's Guide (1st Ed)

In Search of Recovery Workbook: A Christian Man's Guide (1st Ed)

In Search of Recovery: Clinical Guide

Why Is My Partner Sexually Addicted? Insight women Need (1st Ed)

Recovery from Sexual Addiction: A Man's Guide (2nd Ed.)

Recovery from Sexual Addiction: A Man's Workbook (2nd Ed.)

Clinical Guide for the Treatment of Male Sexual Addiction

Sexual Addiction: Understanding and Treatment:
*   Textbook and Reference Manual*

What a Woman Needs to Know about Sexual Addiction (2nd Ed.)

What a Woman Needs to Know about Sexual Addiction (3nd Ed.)

The WHY Book

The FREEDOM Book from Sexual Addiction (Currently not in print)

Recovery from Sexual Addiction: A Path to Sexual Recovery (3rd Ed.)

To contact Paul Becker and or to purchase a book, my e-mail is:
Pbecker11@hotmail.com

Books can also be purchased on Amazon.com

(or many other vendors).

Enter Paul Becker, LPC into the Amazon browser

Preface

Men and women brains are not alike! Their genes cast the sexes quite differently. Men and women brains are not alike! Their genes cast them quite differently. The differences are amazing.

- A man is: fact, logic, and solution oriented. That is as far as he wants to go with any relationship or marriage issues.

- Women, on the other hand, could care less about fact, logic, and solutions. She is relational, value-orientated, and needs to hear what is going on in her partner's life. She also needs to talk about her day and the activities of their children.

- Listen to two women talk, is their conversation relational, value-orientated or fact, logic statement, or solution?

- Men are right brained. That means the right side of their brain generates communication. Since men are right-brained, would it be logical for women to be left brained? Not surprisingly, they are left brained. However, there is a significant addition.

- Women are both left and right brained, and both sides of their brain communicate! Later in the book, the phenomena of compartmentalization are presented. Some hold dual brain communication allows women to function in a broader context of human relations.

But how does brain difference play out in the marital relationship? For starters, each day, men use about 12,000 words, whereas women use at least 24,000 words. So, when her partner arrives home from work, and she asks, "How did your day go, honey." He replies, "Fine." She replies, "No, I mean, did everything go well for you today?" He replies, "It went great; what else do you want to know?" He is done talking; he has used-up his words for the day. She, on the other hand, has plenty of unused words.

She is frustrated.

This story features a wife starved for interaction and an uninterested husband. He has his head buried in the newspaper. The most he has to say is, "What's for dinner?"

What is the solution?

Later in the book, non-sexual intimacy is discussed in detail. It calls for interaction between partners. The above story is a great opportunity for non-sexual intimacy. A wise husband puts aside 15 to 20 minutes to share his day and to listen to his partner. He doesn't need to talk much. If he uses, reflective listening, he's home free. (When using reflective listening, the listener coveys an understanding of the speaker's idea, then offers the idea back to the speaker to confirm the idea is understood).

From the man's point of view, if in the evening he is upset when she says she has a headache, he can't understand why she has so many headaches.

He does not have a clue. Why are men clueless?

Sharing the significant differences between men and woman's brains highlights the difficulties found in many marriages.

When the male is sexually addicted, he wants a fix and feels his wife is being mean when she says, "I have a headache." He desires marital sex and feels deprived when "no" is the outcome of keeping his head in the newspaper!

If only he had a clue?

It is relatively impossible for a woman to understand male sexual addiction, particularly if the husband of her dreams is afflicted. Her mind works differently.

Keep this in mind, and you read this book.

Table of Contents

A woman rarely needs to understand the origin and consequences of male sexual addiction until someone close is found to exhibit addictive sexual behaviors. Each chapter reveals aspects of sexual addiction, all to help a woman decide how she will live after disclosure of her partner's addiction.

Chapter 9 explores the components of Pornography and sexual addiction.

Chapter 10 presents the elements of the recovery journey.

Chapter 11 presents two stories of transformed lives from addiction to recovery.

Appendix A enumerates multiple aberrant sexual behaviors practiced by men.

Appendix B provides literary resources about sexual addiction.

Appendix C guides counseling and Twelve-step Programs.

Note: Named persons in this book have been changed to maintain their confidentiality.

Introduction

Why should I read this book?

When you discovered your partner's secret life of sexual behavior, you were:

- Devastated, outraged, and sad.
- You are concerned about the future of your marriage.
- You are baffled how your partner could betray the family.
- I had many questions about sexual addiction.

This book was written for you. It will give you:

- An understanding of sexual addiction.
- A comprehension of how and why your partner became sexually addicted.
- An explanation of the devastating nature of pornography.
- An answer to the question, what role did I play in fostering my partner's addiction?
- Insights into how your partner rationalized his secret behavior while occupying the marriage bed.
- Insight into what it is like for your partner to live a sexually addicted life.
- An explanation of the difficulty your partner has in ending his addictive behavior.
- A foundation of knowledge to live a recovery journey (if you choose) with your partner.

- An appreciation of living a new life as an outcome of recovery.

Is this book just for partners? No, this book is also a valuable resource for a significant other such as who need answers;

- The mother or grandmother who needs to know why addiction is part of the family.
- Teenage or adult children who need an understanding of addiction and family dynamics to avoid further multi-generational addictive behavior.
- Friends and members of the community to support the addict in his recovery;
- A clergy person who is called upon to counsel partners in marriages affected by sexual addiction.
- Therapists and medical doctors who offer this book to clients as a beginning recovery step.

This book addresses these subjects and much more. It is intended to guide you during difficult times with knowledge to make decisions regarding your life and that of your family.

The real act of marriage takes place in the heart, not in the ballroom or church or synagogue. It's a choice you make—not just on your wedding day, but over and over again—and that choice is reflected in the way you treat your husband or wife.

Barbara

Angelis

Chapter One

Sexual Addiction & Marriage

Choice

Rare the partner who is not outraged when she discovers her husband's secret aberrant sexual behavior. Her trauma and emotions may include:

- Confusion, anger, sadness, shame, and embarrassment.
- Shattered trust.
- Complete confusion—how could her partner do this to their family.
- Incredulous that he was able to keep his secrets so long.
- How could he have lived a dual life in her presence?
- Relieved to learn, she was not crazy for suspecting her partner's aberrant behavior.

- Confounded that he could engage in aberrant behavior, while at the same time, participate in the fruits of the marital bed.
- Fear for her and her family's future—the possibility of living alone, shattered dreams, financial insecurity, loss of friends, and community support.
- The fear she may have contributed to his addiction (You did not).
- Do I know this man?

The reactions a woman experiences upon discovery of her man's secrets could fill many pages. She may be so outraged that her immediate thoughts include divorce. However, most women are simply too traumatized to make a rational decision at the time of discovery. Ultimately, she will have to choose to proceed with a divorce or support her partner's recovery. It is not for this author to make a recommendation.

The solution for each couple may be different.

Likely, her partner is experiencing similar emotions and reactions, but not nearly as traumatic. For men who are discovered, an early reaction is, "How could I have been so stupid?" Another early reaction is fear of losing his addiction, and family—his partner and the children.

Some men are not ready to give up their best friend—their addictive behavior. Recovery takes time for most men. While most men are consumed with shame, many are still paralyzed as to how to end their addictive behavior.

More advice includes:

✓ Do not make hasty decisions; far too much is at stake. Tell your children you and their father are having difficulties, but neither nor their father will let the difficulties change the love you and he has for them.

✓ Do not use the children as sounding boards or a way to punish your partner. Remember, children, especially young children, will conclude that they played a role in the family's problem and blame themselves. Involving children in the man's sexual addiction problem is a form of abuse. Children should not be subjected to this trauma.

✓ Suspend marital relations. If it is not convenient for your partner to sleep in a different bedroom during this period, it may be prudent for him to live outside the home for a while. Use the time of suspended marital relations to get to know each other better and to form a friendship that is likely absent from your marriage today.

✓ Seek counseling for yourself. It is impossible for you to process what is happening in a rational way when you are angry, confused, and in great pain. Of course, therapy is for your partner as well.

✓ Although it is essential for your partner to obtain counseling, you do not have ultimate control over what he decides to do. However, you may wish to insist he pursue counseling in any case.

✓ Join a woman's support group such as S-Anon. You may feel very alone in your anger or grief. A support group will give you the reassurance you are far from alone in dealing with your partner's sexual behavior. It is prudent for you and your partner to enter marital therapy about four to six months from the beginning of his addiction therapy. For now, it is more important for your partner to understand the origin and consequences of addiction and what a recovery journey would look like for him.

✓ Do not manipulate the family bank accounts. While you may wish to protect yourself, until you are in a position to make a rational decision about the future of your marriage, this is not the time to take precipitous action. Do obtain copies of bank and investment statements, etc. so, if needed, a base point can be established. However, you may wish to consult an attorney if your partner is using family funds to pay for his addiction.

✓ If your partner has been arrested for his sexual behavior, do not make any long-term decisions until after the legal proceedings are completed. Your partner is traumatized. He cannot accept more on his plate until the legal proceedings have ended. In cases involving children, the Child Protective Service will determine whether your partner should leave the family home.

Questions about your Partner's Sexual Addiction.

Perhaps you have questions about your partner's sexual addiction. Here are questions often asked by a partner when she comes in for a joint counseling session.

- **What was my role in my partner's addiction?**

It would be rare for a partner or significant other to cause a male to become sexually addicted. While it is possible for a male to become sexually addicted as an adult, the overwhelming majority of men who become addicted find the roots of their addiction in their childhood. Almost with certainly, you did not cause your partner's sexual addiction.

Some still look to themselves for answers to their role in their man's addiction. In his book, *Breaking Free,* Russell Willingham (1999), addresses the partner's role.

> [T]he spouse of a sex addict usually assumes that her husband's behavior is a result of some lack on her part, 'If I were only more interested in sex or lost some weight or tried to be more understanding,' she reasons', 'then surely he wouldn't be doing this.'

What she doesn't understand is that sex addiction is never about the wife; it is about the husband. I am not saying that she does not influence her husband's behavior; I am saying that the issue of sexual brokenness is a lot bigger than that.

- **A genuine sex addict is dealing with issues that predate his wife. Therefore, since she is not the cause, she cannot be the cure.**

Some women resist the idea that their husband's struggle is not their responsibility. They believe that if they could discover the right key to unlock the door, their partner would come around.

One woman in our group went on a campaign to win back her sexually addicted husband by performing all kinds of sexual exploits. She did everything her husband asked, even subjecting herself to things that were painful and humiliating. After all this, he was still not satisfied. Only then did she realize that it was not in her power to change him.

- **Can my partner be cured?**

Many therapists believe that the word "cured" is not applicable to sexual addiction. "Cured" assumes your partner will reach a level of recovery, which will preclude temptation and any form of sexually acting-out behavior—including sexual thinking or fantasy. While your partner can choose to change his behavior, recovery is a life-long journey. The moment a man believes he is "cured," he is on the precipice of a relapse. The good news is, he can live a life-long commitment to forgo his addictive behavior, but the commitment is renewed often.

- **How long will my partner take to end his acting-out behavior?**

Some men can end acting-out behavior quickly. However, for many, it will take a longer period. Each man is unique; each man came out of childhood with varying degrees of brokenness. Experience confirms a rough correlation between the degree of brokenness your partner experienced during childhood and his ability to give-up his addictive behavior. If your partner experienced prolonged and perverse sexual physical, and emotional abuse, the damage is deep; recovery will not be quick.

Dr. Patrick Carnes(1991) research and considerable clinical experience postulate thirty specific recovery tasks, including individual and group counseling, working the Twelve-steps program and involving the family in the recovery program.

John Bradshaw (1988) proposes three stages of recovery. In the first stage, the addict addresses primary addiction. In the second, he addresses codependency. In the third he will get in-touch with feelings, forgiveness, and working on the inner child. In the final stage, he addresses a spiritual awakening and empowerment. Both men agree that recovery can be a long process.

- **How will I know when I can trust my partner?**

As time goes on, you will get a sense of the progress that your partner is making. Only you own the key to allow yourself to trust him. Having said that, suggest you look forward to the time when you and your children are the principal focus of your partner's attention. An addicted man, almost by definition, is very self-centered, but this can change through therapy. If you see, let us say over six months, your partner's attention to family affairs has significantly changed; perhaps it is time to reciprocate with limited trust.

- **Will my partner slip up on his commitment to sexual sobriety?**

A difference exists between one-time or infrequent slips and repetitive slips. A one-time slip means that your partner needs to mount his sobriety horse and continue his ride. Multiple back-to-back slips require him to reenter or continue therapy.

- **What else needs to be done?**

Since partners often lack marital skills, marital therapy is recommended by Carnes and Bradshaw. It is unlikely that parents taught either of you adequate marital skills. For the sake of the marriage and in anticipation of a happy post-addiction life, it is never too late for partners to take time to learn.

Often, courting/dating couples begin sexual activity before they have invested in friendship. Once sexual activity begins the process of getting to know the partner's personhood ends and the focus becomes one of playing house. Marital relations need to be interrupted long enough to allow the partners to finish the natural part of relationship building—getting to know the soul of each other to build a mutual friendship. Couples therapy may help this process. I recommend finding a therapist who uses *Sound Marital House*, or *Imago Therapy*, by John Gottman, Ph.D. or *Getting the Love You Want*, by Harville Hendrix, Ph.D.

- **What can I do to cope with my partner's addiction?**

Find a support group (S-Anon) for women who, like you, are struggling with the pain of their man's addiction. It is important for you to reject any shame you feel and understand your partner has a "cancer" of the soul, and only the treatment he chooses to internalize will make a difference. (Appendix D offers multiple twelve-step programs for partners of sexually addicted men).

Other Fundamentals a Spouse
Needs to Know about Sex Addiction

The remainder of this chapter explores other factors that are at work in your relationship with your partner. They include codependency, compartmentalization, disclosure, and control. Do the descriptions apply to you? Some will apply, but some may not.

Codependency

Is your relationship with your partner codependent?

- At times, do you feel you are married to a boy rather than an adult?

- At times, do you feel you are your partner's mother?

- Do you have a mental list of characteristics you would like to see your partner change?

- Have you tried to counsel your partner on changes the two of you could make to improve your marital relationship with little or no success?

- Do you find your partner gets upset when you make suggestions?

- Do either or both of you tend to avoid dealing with the present moment by using alcohol, drugs, food, sleep, or other distractions?

- Does your partner complain about how you keep the house, fix the family food, spend money, or otherwise about how you behave?

- Do you find that both of you seek to control decisions in your

  relationship?

- When you are away from your partner, does he complain or get angry over the amount of time you were away?

- Do you wish that your relationship with your partner could be more intimate in a non-sexual way?

- Does your partner lack close male friends?

- Is your partner addicted to you? (Demands sex beyond reasonable expectations.)

If you answered yes to at least half of these questions, likely you are in a codependent relationship with your partner. Chapter 8 explores codependency as it affects marriage, where the male is sexually addicted. A woman finds it difficult to understand how a man can engage in sexual behavior (act out) while, at the same time, participate in a marital relationship.

- A woman sees acting out in any form as an assault on the marriage bond.
- She sees acting-out behavior as incredibly selfish.
- She cannot understand how acting out, and a strong marital relationship can exist side by side.

The answer lies in understanding **compartmentalization**. A man sees his world as containing multiple boxes. In one box, he places his marital relationship, in another box, he houses his job, in another box, he places his friends and pastime activities, and in the last box, he hides his sexual addiction. For him, all the boxes are independent, and none touches each other. For example, he does not see how his addiction could affect his job or how acting out could be an affront to his wife. In most cases, his addictive behavior began many years before his relationship with you. By the time he married, he had convinced himself his aberrant sexual behaviors would go away once he married. He was wrong. It just does not happen that way. A woman, on the other hand, understands the components her partner puts in his boxes. However, for her, all the components are lodged in one box. She sees very clearly that when her partner seeks intimacy outside the marriage bed, he depletes intimacy from the marriage. To her, it could not be any clearer.

A Sex Addicted Man's Compartmentalized Brain Boxes

Work Interests	Relationship with Partner	Hobbies, friends, Sports	Sexually Acting out
Box One	Box Two	Box Three	Box Four

A Woman's Integrated Brain Box

Work <-----> Relationship
with partner <---->
Hobbies, sports, friends <--
--> Marital relations

- How a woman sees the world is more realistic.
- During recovery, a perceptive man will see the world as you do.
- He will understand that intimacy outside the marriage bed will destroy the marriage relationship.
- The subject matter in each box is interrelated.
- **To her, it could not be any clearer.**

Disclosure

Invariably questions about disclosure of the man's acting-out behavior must be addressed. It is likely because you are reading this book; you already know some of your partner's story. You may not know it all—and perhaps you have concluded you do not need to know it all at this time—or ever.

Some therapists believe that a fundamental principle of recovery is total honesty and openness in the marriage. They argue, unless disclosure is complete, secrets remain which will distance the partners. Other therapists believe while disclosure is ideal, at times full disclosure will cause unnecessary pain to the partner or significant other. An addicted man may want to disclose his secrets to his partner or significant other, not for the sake of healing the marriage, but to free himself from the burden of housing his secrets and to purge his conscience. In this type of disclosure, the addicted man is disclosing his secrets to reduce his pain, not to establish an honest and intimate relationship.

In a codependent relationship where the female partner or significant other plays the role of the parent and feels that it is her responsibility to fix her spouse, the information he discloses may be used to chastise him. For instance, Nancy badgered Tim for more details about his affairs. Each time he gave her more details, she screamed that he was not telling her everything and she could never trust him again. Disclosure in a codependent relationship often continues an unbalanced relationship. It may be wise to address codependency either in individual or in marital counseling.

Disclosure of the events that occurred before the marriage relationship can be helpful if restricted to appropriate detail. Even information about the current acting-out behavior needs to be shared in appropriate detail. Some disclosures may require detail, but others may not. Disclosure of inappropriate detail may cause significant pain for both the addict as well as the partner or significant other. For example, it is unlikely the partner or significant other needs to know precisely how the masseuse gave her partner oral sex. The fact that he went to a massage parlor should be enough information.

Jane insisted on total detail—of everything that happened. Jane's purpose was not to move on with life but to stoke her anger. The grosser the details she heard, the greater her disdain grew for her partner. She insisted on carrying the heavy load of anger when she could have opted for forgiveness. Forgiveness dispels the anger to which Jane has become addicted.

Disclosure creates mental images that may or may not be accurate. Taking information and creating one's own story usually distorts reality, is unhealthy, and creates undue pain. Disclosure can be both a blessing and a curse.

Disclosure is best undertaken in the presence of a trained therapist who can put boundaries around appropriate detail and share insights from years of experience.

An article entitled, *Surviving Disclosure of Infidelity: Results of an International Survey of 164 Recovering Sex Addicts and Partners* concluded:

- Disclosure is often a process, not a one-time event even in the absence of relapse, withholding of information is common.
- Initial disclosure usually is most conducive to healing the relationship in the end when it includes all the major elements of the acting-out behaviors but avoids the 'gory details.'
- Over half the partners threatened to leave after disclosure, but only one-quarter of couples separate.

- Half the sex addicts reported one or more major slips or relapses, which necessitated additional decisions about disclosure.
- Neither disclosure nor threats to leave prevented relapse.
- With time, 96% of addicts and 93% of partners came to believe that disclosure had been the right thing.
- Partners need support from professionals and peers during the process of disclosure.
- Honesty is a crucial healing characteristic.
- The most helpful tools for coping with the consequences of addiction are counseling and Twelve Step programs.
- Disclosure, threats to leave, and relapses are parts of the challenge of treating and recovering from, addictive disorders (Schnider, Corley & Irons, 1998).

Control

For the addicted man, childhood was a time when his need for emotional nourishment was stifled. For example, your partner, as a child, may have been revered only because he demonstrated good behavior or for his high-level performance in school or sports, but not because he was a child who was entitled to be loved. Consequently, the child learned he could control his environment through his performance. He learned that if he were a "responsible" child, the possibility of a favorable parental response was greater.

Other consequences of being overly responsible include a focus on being serious, overly self-reliant, unable to trust, and an inability to relax. Paradoxically, he learned he could control what he did with his own body. He found when he felt sad, put upon, inferior, or did not measure up to parental expectations; he could escape his environment by fantasy and masturbation to achieve euphoria associated with stimulation. He learned, while his parents did not provide the nourishment he needed for emotional growth, he did control an important element of his world that guaranteed good feelings. Continued repetition of good feelings led to a habit and ultimately, sexual addiction. Again, paradoxically, he learned he had to be in control to manage his environment.

You can testify to the control an addicted man demands in marriage. For example, he may want to have marital relations on his timetable rather than by a shared loving agreement to celebrate the marriage bed. Males often   want family member behavior to match their standards or expectations. He wants what he wants when he wants it. Addicts learn to repeat self-centered behavior, that is, to love a partner and children based on their performance.

As a child, he was robbed of good parental role models. Now, not only is he sexually addicted but his role as a spouse and parent is likely deficient.

Codependency, disclosure, compartmentalization, and control need to be addressed in therapy—often by both partners.

Are all the descriptors of male sexual addiction negative? There is hope for recovery. An important element is a capacity for the partners to live at a level which provides opportunities to engage in non-sexual intimacy daily. This is called "living at 40" and is addressed in Chapter 7.

**Don't let life discourage you;
everyone who got where
he is had to
begin where he was.**

Richard L. Evans

Chapter Two

Sexual Addiction from a Clinical Perspective

Sex Addicts Anonymous (SAA), a Twelve-Step program like Alcoholics Anonymous (AA), is a fellowship of men and women who share their experiences, strength, and hope with each other, so they may overcome their addiction and help others recover from sexual addiction or dependency. As a beginning, we will use their definition of sexual addiction.

What is sexual addiction?

Sex Addiction can involve a wide variety of practices. Sometimes an addict has trouble with just one unwanted behavior, sometimes with many. Many sex addicts say their unhealthy use of sex has been a progressive process. It may have started with an addiction to masturbation, pornography (either printed or electronic), or a relationship, and over the years progressed to increasingly dangerous behaviors.

The essence of all addiction is the addict's experience of powerlessness over a compulsive behavior, which results in their lives becoming unmanageable. The addict is out of control and experiences tremendous shame, pain, and self-loathing. The addict may wish to stop—yet repeatedly fails to do so. The unmanageability of an addict's life can be seen in the consequences he suffers. He may lose relationships, have difficulties with work, arrests, financial troubles, a loss of interest in things not sexual, low self-esteem and despair.

> Sexual preoccupation takes tremendous amounts of energy. As the addict's preoccupation grows, a pattern of behavior (or rituals) follows, which usually leads to acting out (for some it is flirting, searching the *net* for pornography, or driving to the park). "When the acting out happens, there is a denial of feelings usually followed by despair and shame or a feeling of hopelessness and confusion" (Sex Addicts Anonymous, 2009).

Several terms from this definition as well as a few additional characteristics of addiction need a closer look.

Acting out

Throughout this book, the term "acting out" is used in place of naming a specific sexual behavior. It is used as a category of behaviors practiced by addicted men.

Paul Becker, LPC and Mary Lou Swanberg, CHPS

Wide variety of behaviors

Sexual behaviors tend to fall into two broad categories. The first category includes illegal behaviors—and fall under the rubric of sexual offenses.

Some examples of illegal sexual behaviors include:

- Voyeurism;
- Child pornography;
- Pedophilia;
- Stalking; and
- Professional misconduct.

Examples of sexual behaviors that are toxic to the sex addict but are not regarded as illegal include:

- Compulsive sear images on the Internet;
- searching for stimulating pornographic
- Compulsive masturbation;
- Multiple affairs;
- Frequent use of paper and video pornography;
- Multiple or anonymous partners include safe sex;
- Phone sex;
- Use of chat rooms to stimulate thinking, fantasy, and sexual behavior (cybersex);
- Voyeurism (non-criminal);
- Frequenting strip clubs;
- Sexual massage and lap dancing, sans "happy endings;" and
- Prostitution (Illegal in most states but not considered an offense in many jurisdictions.)

The above lists are not exhaustive; several other sexual behaviors can become addictive. (Appendix A provides a comprehensive description of addictive behaviors practiced by sex addicts.)

Denial

Accepting, "I am a sexually addicted man," is frightening and has consequences. When a man admits he has a problem, he is saying to himself, "The most pleasurable activity in my life must end." That is not easy. It is quite common for a man to deny he has a serious acting-out problem. At times, the response is some form of, "How can I have my cake and eat it too?"

Shame plays a pivotal role in denial, as well. To the sexually addicted man, living as an alcoholic or a drug addict seems to be a far better alternative. Some equate sex addiction with people who are "perverted." It is difficult for a man to accept he is a sex addict.

For the most part, a man in denial believes:

- I am just a man. It is what I do.
- It is not so bad.
- I work hard and deserve some pleasure.
- I can stop it whenever I want—just not right now.
- I have a stronger libido than the average man.
- If I thought I was hurting somebody, I would do something about it.

Our society exaggerates the importance of sex in the movies, on television, the Internet, and even at the Super Bowl. Yet, when a man admits his sexual appetites are out of control, that same society looks at him, askew. Our society seems to say, it is okay for you to go into the candy store, but if we catch you eating any of the goodies, we will ostracize you. In this environment, how could a man feel safe to admit he has a serious problem? Denial seems to be the way out for many.

Powerlessness over a compulsive behavior

All addictions share the same characteristic of powerlessness over compulsive behavior. It means your partner, despite many pledges to the contrary to himself and others, is unable to reject all temptations to act out. He may be sexually sober for periods or may be able to avoid certain practices, but he finds himself repeating sexual behaviors of choice, even when he would prefer to stop his acting-out behavior.

Let's consider Vince's compulsive behavior

Vince is a very successful salesperson of medical products. His territory covers several northwestern States. He travels from city to city and from hospital to hospital. Vince relishes his job because it allows him to engage in sexual stimulation with no expectation of being caught. His fetish is an adult or erotic bookstore where "peep" shows are featured. The "peep" shows foster stimulation followed by masturbation either alone or with another man.

While he knows his line of medical products well, he understands his sales presentation is critical to closing a deal. He finds sexual stimulation before meeting with a client, calms him down and allows him to think straight, he said, "Orgasm reduces my anxiety of meeting with people." He was working on a new account at a large hospital in South Dakota. He put many hours into presenting the benefits of his products and socializing with his clients. He expected that after his next meeting with hospital administrators, they would decide to move their business to his company. He was very excited. The new business from this hospital would put him over his annual sales quota.

Vince set a meeting with the hospital administrator for three o'clock on Friday afternoon. He spent the morning reviewing data sheets and other material he needed for his presentation. After lunch and before the meeting he took a taxi to an adult bookstore on the other side of town. He engaged in his normal stimulation activities. He noticed another man who showed considerable interest in his activities. After talking with this man, Vince agreed to go to his apartment nearby.

The excitement of the moment fed into a trance-like state and Vince lost track of time. By the time he ended his liaison with his newfound companion, the meeting time at the hospital had passed. He called the hospital administrator to apologize, but the administrator had gone home for the weekend.

Vince gave up significant financial remuneration for the sake of short-term sexual pleasure. Vince was powerless over his compulsive behavior. While Vince felt shame and remorse for his behavior, it did not stop him from engaging in similar behavior in other cities he visited.

Addicts experience psychological pain and self-loathing

Psychological pain is often a consequence of addiction. You may wonder how a man experiences pain when his compulsive behavior is intended to be pleasurable. Orgasm is pleasurable, but the self-loathing that follows is not.

Your partner probably appears to be reasonably normal in many ways. Paradoxically, your partner may not even realize the extent of his distress because it is how he has lived most of his life, that is, in low-grade depression. Often it is only in therapy where the man gains insights into his underlying discontent. The addicted man rarely has a clue on how to experience joy, happiness, and a fulfilled life. His reality is acting out in secret.

The man will expend considerable energy hiding his sexual behavior and his pain. Picture your partner's right hand fully extended with his palm forward and his left hand back by his left ear, palm forward. The right hand symbolizes the effort to which he will go to project the image of a well-adjusted, healthy person. Often, he will demonstrate over-achievement in his work, involvement in his church, and other pretenses he believes will make him look good. His right hand is a mask that hides the person who he would like others to believe is his real self. He believes the real self is his left hand. The left hand symbolizes his self-loathing, lack of self-esteem, and profound shame related to his behavior, and other negative thought processes. He believes he is worthless and mired in so much sin that there is little or no hope for him — the left-hand lives in constant pain and self-loathing.

Sean illustrates the consequences of living a dual life.

Sean was a high-level executive. He rose through the ranks quickly and had major responsibilities. He was well respected by top-level management and by his peers. He seemed to have it all. He had a good analytical mind and was able to keep many projects going simultaneously. He had a unique way of keeping his subordinate managers loyal and interested in his game plan.

Those who knew him were shocked when they read in the newspaper that he was arrested for stalking a young woman. He explained to his therapist that he lived a dual life. While he had done well in business, he attributed his success to luck. On the other hand, he felt he was a total failure as a husband and father. He despised the fact he was unable to resist temptation. He feared he was intrinsically evil and perhaps possessed. Sean, who lives in both his right and left-handed worlds, ultimately must face his demons.

A clinical term conceptualizes the discordance a man experiences when he lives simultaneously in two conflicting mental constructs. It is called cognitive dissonance. The condition can be resolved by recognizing the reality of his stress-induced state. However, frequently, the man continues to live with cognitive dissonance because he believes an underlying premise that he is evil while he is trying to deceive the world with his "good guy" act. Unfortunately, the cognitive dissonance, to which an addicted man subscribes, fosters living in low-grade depression. An addicted man acts out to self-medicate the pain he experiences when life is full of negative vibes.

Representations of the right and the left hands are exaggerations. The addicted man is neither as good as he would have others believe nor is he as evil, as he believes his left hand symbolizes. The "real" self requires both hands to be congruent. He admits that his right hand is a mask against letting the world see his addiction. He must recast the concepts of both his right and left hand. Moreover, he must admit to himself that God does not make junk. He is not a dreg. When both hands are congruent, he is in the position to begin the work that will lead to a healthy lifestyle and to end his self-loathing.

Unmanageability—out of control

Most addicts have a limited intellectual understanding of the consequences of pursuing acting-out behavior. Their intellectual understanding and behavior are often at odds. For example, a man in counseling expressed his understanding that if he views pornography on a company computer, loss of job and income could result. Nevertheless, he and many others continue to view pornography on a work computer. Once a man begins to ruminate over the images he expects to see on the Internet, he enters a trance-like state where all consequences are ignored.

A man in therapy is introduced to the concept that pornography and masturbation rob him of the capacity to be emotionally intimate in his marriage—often a difficult concept for addicts to internalize. A man often reverts to the emotional state created when first introduced to unwanted sexual behavior or material (e.g., pornography, erotic videos, etc.). The man seeks to repeat the high he experienced, that is, the arousal connected with his first childhood exposure. Despite his intellectual knowledge, he may continue to seek stimulation outside the marriage. He is out of control.

Jeff illustrates what it means to be sexually out of control

Jeff reported he spent $60,000 for online pornography, massage parlors, and travel to engage in extramarital affairs. He said he knew it was only a matter of time before the financial consequences would take their toll on his business and family. While he hoped he would not be caught, he admitted to the possibility.

Jeff entered therapy at the insistence of his spouse to deal with outbursts of anger in the home. Jeff believed his outbursts were justified. He said, "If only I would get the respect I deserved from my wife and children, my anger would be history!"

During therapy, his therapist helped him to see that the underlying reason for his anger was the lack of self-respect he had for himself, which was related to his hidden sexual behavior. He told his therapist he did not want to deal with his sexual behavior, only his anger

Jeff chose to quit therapy. He continued his angry outbursts in the home and his sexual quests outside the home. Jeff was not ready to deal with his behavior and its consequences.

In search of the Holy Grail

An addicted man is never satisfied with his latest affair, massage, or the intensity of the pornography he finds online. This characteristic of sexual addiction is called "progression." Sex and its pursuit do not fill the hole in the man's soul. In group counseling, a man who pursues multiple partners reports that he gets bored. He finds shortcomings in his victim, which he then uses to justify terminating the affair. While a man may continue an affair for several years, and even marry one of his partners, this is not the norm. Progression is never being satisfied with yesterday's sexual exploitation; the addict always needs more and different.

Jacob's story is one of never being satisfied.

Jacob is a well-built and handsome man. As a teenager, both his contemporaries and older women found him attractive. He was never at a loss for a date and sexual gratification. In his late twenties, he saw his other male friends settle down and take on family responsibilities. He envied his friends since none of his relationships lasted more than six months. He began to date Susan. Susan was different from any of his other conquests. She seemed to understand him and truly care for him. They married. Shortly after the wedding vows were exchanged, Susan became pregnant. Their son was only two months old when she discovered that Jacob had engaged in affairs, one while they were dating and a second while she was pregnant.

She told Jacob she would leave him unless he entered therapy. During therapy, Jacob talked about the great thrill he experienced during the pursuit of a new conquest. "The conquest is everything for me," he said, "Once I seduce my conquest, I quickly lose interest—no more challenge."

Jacob said he loved Susan, but felt she was unreasonable to expect him to give up that which satisfied him most in life. He said, "My life would just not be worth much if I could not pursue women." He talked about finding the perfect woman, the one that would quell his quest. He said, "At one time I felt Susan would be my perfect woman. I was disappointed when Susan did not turn out to meet my expectations." During the time Jacob was in therapy, he met another woman from his office who seemed to be interested in him.

Jacob terminated therapy, and Susan divorced him.

Neither Jacob nor any other addicted man can become permanently satisfied in their pursuit of illicit sex. A man cannot find the Holy Grail in sex.

Sex addiction cycle

An addicted man has a sex-addiction cycle and uses rituals to lay the foundation for acting-out behavior.

Picture a clock:

- At **noon** (top of the clock), a man experiences an acting-out trigger. For example, one man's trigger is an attack on his integrity or self-worth or if he perceives a complaint about his work. His perception will trigger a negative reaction and mood change. It is a feeling of depressed mood.

- **At fifteen after the hour**, he begins to medicate his negative feelings by escaping reality. For example, he may engage in a fantasy, or think about a past sexual encounter.

- **At 30 minutes after the hour**, he begins an acting-out ritual. The acting-out ritual is a series of actions or behaviors that result in mental and physical arousal. Arousal leads to orgasm.

- **At 45 minutes after the hour**, the addict experience's shame, guilt, and self-loathing from having acted out. He may minimize his actions and promise himself not to repeat his acting-out behavior. However, the transitory guilt passes, and he returns to the top of the clock, eventually to begin another cycle.

The addicted man may have different triggers that begin his acting-out cycle. He always has multiple rituals. The concept is the same. The major variation is the amount of time between the repetitions of his cycle. A man believed reduced frequency (what was daily is now weekly) represents recovery. While he is making limited progress, lasting progress means eliminating the acting-out cycle.

Acting-Out Ritual

In phase three of the *Sex Addiction Cycle*, every addict repeats an acting-out ritual. Acting-out rituals are a series of events or thoughts that the addict steps through before engaging in sexual activity. The addict needs to get in touch with his acting-out ritual and identify at what point the ritual can be stopped. The addict needs to apply an interdiction to change the sexual response.

According to Carnes (1994):

> The ritual seems magical to bring order out of chaos. Think of it as a dance---certain steps, certain sounds, ceremony, rhythm, special artifacts--which can be very elaborate but have one purpose: to put addicts into another world so they can escape the conditions of real life over which they think they have no control. Fantasy is compounded by delusion at this point, for the mood-altered state is a world in which the addict no longer cares about control in the same way. Sexual obsession is pursued to its peak regardless of risk, harm, or other consequences. There is only one kind of control that matters now; control of sexual pleasure. Once they start dancing, they rarely, if ever, can stop on their own.

Mason shares his acting-out ritual

> I know the location of all the strip bars in the city. I cruise neighborhoods nearby, tell myself I was not going near a strip club, but find as part of

my ritual repeatedly parking nearby. Eventually, a channel will provide the visual stimulation For others, the rituals may include visiting parks, the back seat of a car, the living room couch, swimming pools, shopping malls, restrooms, movie theaters, internet, porn shops, peep shows, or other locations that are part of the pattern used to set the stage for acting out. The TV remote is a curse for many. Channel flipping can be compared to having a gun with one round in the needed to activate the lust pattern.

Addicts are not cognizant of the consistency of their ritualization patterns until they are asked to record the events that lead to an orgasm. They are surprised to discover their ritual often begins long before they take any action. Initial ritual steps may begin with feelings of hunger, anger, loneliness, and tiredness, often referred by the acronym **HALT**. Since addicts frequently live in a state of low-grade depressed mood, the feeling of being emotionally down may trigger their ritual.

Samuel explains his ritual in pursuit of Holy Grail of sex

Samuel had a very stressful job as the Vice President for Production.

I long for the touch of a female. Massage parlors that specialized in oral sex or masturbation are my sexual lifeline. From my point-of-view, the stress of my senior level position entitles me to seek relief from my charged-up daily life. For me, the answer is to go to a massage parlor every Friday afternoon.

Samuel began to realize massage parlors did not make him happy. He constantly looked for a better experience but was never satisfied. Through the help of his counselor, he began to record his acting out rituals. Together they looked for the event or change in mood that began his descent to acting out. Samuel found he could stop mental processing at an initial stage. When skiing, once Samuel was past the initial stages of his descent, he could no longer stop. They called Samuel's descent his slippery slope.

Samuel outlined his *acting-out ritual* in the following steps:

- During the week, Samuel's mind would process past trips to one or more massage parlors. He would think about the woman with the best technique, the woman who satisfied him the most. Thinking about experiences kept his sexual tension high during the week.

- Samuel constantly looked for someone who could excite him more. He tried out new parlors in search of what he called the perfect touch.

- Wednesday's local newspaper contained ads for massage parlors. Samuel waited in anticipation.

- When a new ad appeared, Samuel called for an appointment. He often found new ads.

- Friday mornings were times of very high sexual energy. At times Samuel would masturbate in his office, so the afternoon's experience would last longer.

- Samuel drove his older car to work on Fridays. He thought he was less likely to be identified in his Honda Accord than in his BMW

- Samuel cleared his Friday afternoon calendar to leave the office by 3:00 P.M.

- When Samuel got into his car Friday afternoon, he occasionally had second thoughts, like maybe I can skip it today. He would tell himself that he would go to Starbucks for a coffee. Invariably, he found himself driving through the massage parlor neighborhood, even when he told himself that he was going to Starbucks.

- Samuel went to a massage parlor just about every Friday afternoon. He found he could no longer stop himself.

Samuel must address his rituals. Unless he constructively manages them, he likely will return to his entitlement logic; I deserve this to come down from my charged-up daily life.

Rarely can a man travel the recovery journey unaided by counseling. Group counseling and Twelve-step programs are proven to help the man on his recovery journey.

Secrets

Addiction always includes secrets and lies. The first exposure to unwanted sexual material or behavior usually begins in a secretive environment. A man reports that his experience has taught him that sex is much more exciting when it is secretive and forbidden. A secretive view of sex may communicate other messages. For example, a child learns, in addition to sex, not to speak about other behavioral transgressions he experiences in his family environment.

In her book, *The Sexual Healing Journey: A Guide for Survivors of Sexual Abuse,* Wendy Maltz (2001), says it this way:

Many survivors say secretive, compulsive sexual activity is the most intense and satisfying experience they know. Fear of being caught may increase the adrenaline rush; feeling a chemical high is the secret sex. However, like taking drugs, this high is a trap. To maintain the affair, the compulsive masturbation, the illegal sexual activity, the survivor must lie repeatedly. Viewing sex as secretive can add to shame. This must really be bad if I can't talk about it,' a survivor may think. This kind of sex becomes self-destructive.

A secretive view of sex makes communication about sex impossible. Couples often cannot speak about their real sexual feelings and needs. Because of the lack of open communication, survivors may feel the same as they did in the abuse—all alone during sex.

One would think that a man would seek help at some point. However, experience has taught that nine out of ten seek therapy only after having the most intimate secret discovered. In fact, one man came to therapy only to get his partner off his back.

Jim shows how difficult it is to end his addictive behavior.

Jim was caught downloading pornography at work. It happened several times, and he was suspended from his job. The suspension triggered the discovery of his secrets by his wife. He confessed remorse to both his boss and his wife. At his wife's insistence, Jim sought therapy. He acknowledged he probably spent two or three hours a day seeking erotic images on the Internet. Jim had three young children, and his wife threatened, unless he participated in therapy, she would never allow the children to be alone with him.

Jim continued to harbor his secret. Giving up pornography was too much for Jim. He thought his therapist knew all the ins and outs of Internet pornography. Jim asked his therapist during his second session if there was a way he could continue to download pornography. Jim could not bear the thought of giving up his erotic pornography, his best friend.

Jim's employer transferred him to another part of the country, and it is not known if he was able to address his addictive behavior.

A man like Jim, who enters therapy, finds it very difficult to give up his secret behavior. An addicted man is encouraged to find an accountability partner with whom he can share his intimate secrets and temptations. Coming out of secrecy is perhaps one of the most difficult tasks he faces. Coming out of secrecy is also the first step in recovery.

Even clergy have challenges as Rev. George's story reveals.
Reverend George crashed his computer. He thought it would be a simple fix to restore his computer. He asked a man in his congregation to look at the computer to see if he could get it back up and running. The man found Rev. George's computer crashed because of the vast quantity of pornography he had downloaded to his hard drive.

The man discovered Rev. George's biggest secret. Rev. George was petrified that members of his congregation would learn his secret. He did not know where to turn.

Ultimately, Rev. George chose to commute an hour from his home to join a sex addiction therapy group. In therapy, Rev. George realized that the consequences of not ending his addiction would be the loss of his position and marriage. In due course, Rev. George shared his deepest secret with his wife. Contrary to his expectations, his wife gave him positive support.

He then dared to share his secret with the elders in his church. Again, he was pleasantly surprised that they did not condemn him. To the contrary, the elders praised Rev. George's decision to seek help.

Rev George faced one more hurdle with shedding his toxic secrets. He was challenged to share his addiction and struggle with his men's group at his church. The elders told him that when he is "real" with his flock, he is truly their shepherd. Rev. George reports that overcoming his sexual addiction has made his marriage stronger and much happier. Again, contrary to his expectations, he feels respected by his flock for having come down from his pedestal to share his humanness. Rev. George shared his most shameful secrets. By doing so, he trumped his toxic shame.

Lies addicts tell themselves to justify acting out

The addicted man hides his behavior. He becomes so adept at lying; the distinction between a lie and truth become indistinguishable.

The propensity to lie to avoid feelings of shame often begins in childhood. In short, the child exposed to sex suffers shame. It tells him something is wrong with him. As an adult, his shame fosters a need to hide his behavior, and if he is caught, to blame another person and profess, "It will never happen again." Lying becomes a defense mechanism he uses to hide his embarrassment.

When a child senses something is intrinsically wrong with him as a person, one of his defense mechanisms is to try to convince the world otherwise. For example, a common form of lying for such a child is to exaggerate. The child believes he cannot be loved simply for who he is, so he exaggerates his accomplishments, feelings, and experiences. For the child who will become sexually addicted, his reality is a lie.

Lying becomes part of an addict's being. His ability to lie, and more importantly, his ability to believe his lies, reaches a critical point when he lies to justify his acting-out behavior. Frequently heard from an adult addict include:

- I do not go on my computer other than to check e-mail.
- I have gotten rid of all my porno web sites and magazines.
- I do not need an Internet blocker; I can handle this.
- I plan to quit as soon as my wife goes on the pill.
- There is no way I am going to be caught.
- What I do in the privacy of my bedroom is my business.
- The reason I act out my wife does not need as much sex as I do.
- I am just looking for intellectual stimulation, not sex.

Lying is egregious when it is destructive to the family. Lying as a cover to continue sexual behavior is hitting bottom.

The wife or a significant other, who has just learned about her partner's acting-out behavior, usually can enumerate times when he was lying. Sadly, lying his probably has not ended. It takes time in recovery before the man is willing to face the total reality of his secrets and lies. You are right in wanting to trust your partner but be patient. It will take time.

Multiple addictions

A sexually addicted man frequently has other addictions. In addition to sex, alcohol, drugs, eating, work, gambling, spending money, and, perfectionism are common. Perfectionism is the man's attempt to compensate for his lack of self-esteem. Perfectionism may also influence his expectations of himself, his partner, and his children's performance. These expectations are rarely reasonable.

Alcohol and drugs may be used to facilitate acting out or in response to the shame and guilt of having acted out.

A man who deals with multiple addictions finds it is easier to shed non-sexual addictions. For example, the alcoholic buys a bottle to satisfy his craving. On the other hand, a sex addict satisfies his craving in his head with sexual thoughts. Also, the high he experiences from orgasm is usually more powerful than the high from other addictions.

Compare alcohol and drug addiction to sexual addiction

Someone who is "addicted" to sex will demonstrate a similar brain chemistry response, as does a person dependent on alcohol or drugs.

Male sexual addiction is a preoccupation with build-up and achieving release in the form of an orgasm. The mind of the addicted man becomes conditioned to filter almost all human actions and images through a sexual prism. For example, the addicted man will ogle a woman in the office, on the subway, or walking down the street. He focuses on sexually stimulating body parts. While the obvious—breasts, buttocks, and body curves stimulate sexual thoughts, for some even the curve of an ankle, the length of the neck, and hands, feet, and facial parts are sexually stimulating. An addicted man will open a newspaper or magazine and immediately seek images that stimulate sexual feelings. He lives in a stimulated state for hours each day.

The driving force for an alcohol/drug addict is the need to induce mood alteration by using an external-chemical substance. The alcoholic uses brain chemicals to begin his addictive behavior. Both use mood alteration to deal with the problems that come with life.

The difference between male and female sexual addiction

For the male, stimulation and orgasm are the goals. The source of stimulation can be quite different for each man. However, sexual triggers, in general, lead a man down the path to acting out. Triggers come in the form of actions or mental processing of fantasies or thinking.

On the other hand, for many women, sexual addiction is based on an idealized concept of relationship and love. While some women are addicted to masturbation, many more compulsively seek a "perfect" relationship. Also, a woman may engage in one - night stands to satiate, paradoxically, the pain of childhood abuse. As such, the intended outcome is something other than orgasm.

A man who engages in frequent extramarital affairs usually is not looking for an "ideal" relationship. His product is to seduce and experience sexual pleasure. It is difficult to understand the nature of male sexual addiction; a woman has no way of connecting experientially or intellectually with being driven to repeat orgasm after orgasm.

Sexual addiction begins in childhood

No man wakes up on his 21st birthday and decides to become sexually addicted. For eight out of ten, the roots of addiction come from childhood. Frequently, the addicted adult reports that he was exposed to unwanted sexual material or behavior anywhere from age three to thirteen. Chapter 4 explores in detail the factors that can lead a child to become an addicted adult.

A sexually addicted Christian man

Can a man who puts his sexual needs first, call himself a Christian. You may wonder how your partner participates in church services, Bible studies, and even receives communion while thinking about the next time he can search the Internet for erotic images;

Your question is valid and may even be shared by your partner. He too questions his relationship with God. He too wonders if his behaviors are paving his road to hell. Almost with certainty, your partner does not have a loving relationship with his God. Your partner may not know how a loving relationship with God even looks. A man often takes his semblance of understanding God from his human relationships. Your partner's relationship with his father may have poorly molded his image of God.

The addict's relationship with his parents or caregivers often shapes his understanding of God. Dave's relationship with his father distorted his concept of God.

Dave explains the conflict between worship God or sex

Dave's earliest memory of his Father was his large size and his roar. He had a ritual when he punished Dave and his two older brothers.

As Dad took off his belt, he would tell me; this is going to hurt me more than it is going to hurt you, then wallop me until I screamed in pain. From the first time, I can remember being beaten by Dad; I hated his lie. How could his pain be greater than my pain? He did not have welts on his backside. I also remember wondering why Mom allowed Dad to beat me so bad. She knew. So often the beatings were not deserved.

Good moments to remember about Dad were few. Dad liked to go to the carnival when it came to town. I remember going to the carnival with him and my brother. He began to take us once we were about five years old. I remember getting my face and hands sticky from eating cotton candy. One of my older brothers, Ben, was a little league pitcher. He practiced throwing a ball through a tire hung from a tree and had great accuracy. He would win several stuffed bears until the carnival man chased us away. Ben once gave me a teddy bear that I kept for many years.

Our family attended church, and I saw Dad pray, but I never understood his prayer. He always prayed with his mouth and eyes shut. He never taught me how to pray. Once I asked him about it. His reply was, ask your Mother. I remember thinking prayer never made Dad a nice person. My older brother introduced me to sex when I was about six. He showed me how to make it feel good. I found those feelings helped me to feel better, particularly after Dad beat me. It was my 'secret time' out behind the shed. In time, I became sexually addicted, and I, too, grew into a big man like my father. My 'secret time' never went away, even after I married.

Dave began counseling when his wife, Julie, told him unless he quit yelling at her and spanking, Teddy, their son, she was going to leave and move back with her parents.

Michael, a pastoral counselor, helped Dave explore the connection between his childhood experiences and his adult life. After several months of counseling, he told his counselor about his 'secret time.' I broke down and cried, oh God, where are you when I need you?

Michael, his therapist, asked Dave to describe his God. If Dave reached out to God, to whom was Dave reaching out? **Who was Dave's God**?

Dave shared; I often try to pray. I close my eyes to pray, but **words do not come**. My image of God is of a very large person with mighty hands and a scowling face. I read in the Bible to fear God. I had that down pat. For years, I thought God was extremely angry with me, you know, about my 'secret time.' **I am terrified at the prospect of meeting God when I die.**

Michael asked Dave to contrast the images of his Father and his God. Dave sat still for several minutes. His face became distorted, and he exclaimed, **My God, is just like my father!**

Michael said, Dave if you cry out to an angry God, how do you expect God to nourish you? What do you mean, asked Dave? Michael replied, Dave, your

Father was unable to nourish you in the ways you needed in childhood. If your image of God encompasses the same unpleasant characteristics as your Father, how can you expect to be nourished?

Michael asked, Dave, do need to be nourished by God? Dave cried, yes. Michael said, then let's begin by understanding the incredible love God has for you.

In time, Dave understood God only wants one thing for him, to be his loving Father in heaven, Dave's dearest friend. Dave learned God created him and knew his weaknesses. God understands all of humanity's weaknesses. Jesus was human and divine. By being born, Jesus witnessed first-hand human weakness. This was a comforting realization for Dave.

Dave's 'secret time' was never secret from God. God saw what caused Dave's need for 'secret time,' and God saw the pain it caused in Dave's life.

God cried with Dave, not at him.

Dave is far from alone. You may have said to yourself as you read Dave's story, I know what it is like to feel unloved by my Dad.

When men and women deal with the dysfunction of their childhood, frequently, their image of God resembles the image of their Father. Rarely do they feel the great love God has for them. Many are like Dave. They believe God is angry just as they are angry with themselves and the circumstances they endured during childhood. They have a hole in the cup of their soul for which they seek healing.

What does this story have to do with God? God is everything; an addict's past is not.

God loves, addiction is painful. God wants to be your partner's rock, his foundation. Addiction is now his rock and foundation, his most important need. God wants his life to be of service to others. His addiction keeps him bottled up within himself. God is joy and deserving of praise. Addiction is isolation that keeps your partner from knowing joy.

Without changing his relationship with God, the journey to sexual sobriety is lonely and painful.

In his book, *Breaking Free,* Russell Willingham (1999), says he never met a sex addict who understands God's grace.

> With near certainty, the relationship between an addicted man and his God is lacking. He sees himself as despicable and unlovable. His understanding of God is as perverse as is his fears of the consequences of his addiction. His image of God is totally contrary to the reality of God's love.

As such, he is changing a sex addict's understanding of God from one of vengeance to one of unconditional love is a huge step forward. The addict has lived his life in the belief that he does not deserve God's love.

In Jerry's story, Santa Claus became the image of God.

My image of God was that of a stern Santa Claus who had a big book where He recorded what I had done right or all my many failures. The list of good deeds took one page, whereas my evil endeavors took the rest of the book.

During a religious retreat, I began to comprehend how much God loved me even during my darkest moments. I had moved away from God, but God never moved away from me. This was a life-changing understanding for me. Because of the transformation, I began to understand how I had isolated myself from those I loved because of my addiction. I learned how joyful life could be when I came out of my cave and began to serve others. I began to see I could direct the rays of love God sent my way onto others. I realized my sexual lust brought no joy, only pain. This is the understanding I craved for years but was blind to its reality. This is an alternative journey a sexually addicted man can choose to travel.

Sex addict and sex offender

The predominant behaviors reported by a man who voluntarily enters therapy include compulsive scanning of the Internet for pornographic images; engaging in masturbation, marital affairs, phone sex, frequenting strip bars/lap dancing, and massage parlors. The addicted man and those close to him may fear that he will become a sex offender. A man who practices the above behaviors usually does not cross the line into criminal sex offender behaviors.

It is uncommon for a man who engages in one or more of these behaviors than to abuse children. Most often, the behavior the man finds comforting in adulthood is like the behavior introduced as a child. While many children are abused, most do not become adult abusers of children. On the other hand, a man who goes to prison for child molestation is more likely to have been sexually abused as a child.

In some cases, a man may be tempted to view child pornography. What starts as curiosity may become compulsive. The interest in child pornography usually starts in childhood with some form of sexual interaction with other children or sexual abuse.

Sexually addictive behavior is progressive, both in terms of frequency and intensity. An addicted man has a compulsive need to seek successive highs that are more rewarding. For example, a man addicted to pornography will find the images that once stimulated him are no longer enticing. He will continue to seek more provocative images. Progression also means greater intensity. For example, the addict may find that he may masturbate more. Progression usually does not exceed the man's internal standard of sexual behavior.

It is unlikely that your partner is, or could be, a sex offender, but let us explore the possibility. If you found your partner abused children, should you divorce him and forever separate him from your family? That is a decision you will have to make. However, let us look beyond his possible incarceration and explore the potential danger he will present to your family upon release from prison and after treatment.

A 1994 Department of Justice study followed 272,111 people released from prison in 15 States. Of that number, 9,700 were sex offenders of which nearly 4,300 identified as child molesters. The number represented two-thirds of all sex offenders released from state prisons that year (US Department of Justice, 2003).

This study reported recidivism rates (the percentage of time a former prisoner is rearrested) for **all criminals** as:

- 67.5% were rearrested for a felony or serious misdemeanor within three years.
- 46.9% were reconvicted.
- 25.4% were sentenced to prison for a new crime.

The same Department of Justice study reported that the recidivism rate for **sex offenders** is less. The recidivism rate for all sex offenders who within three years of release committed another sex-based crime was 53 percent (The recidivism rate included men who had committed all forms of sexual offenses).

The recidivism rate for child molesters is lower. The same Department of Justice study found that an estimated 33 percent of the 4,300 released child molesters were rearrested for another sex crime against a child within three years.

The State of Virginia conducted three similar studies and found recidivism rates for sex offenders who were arrested for a subsequent sex crime are around 8 percent. The three State of Virginia studies followed a "cohort," that is, all sex offenders released from prison during successive three-year study periods (recidivism in Virginia, 2001, 2003, & 2005).

One of your primary considerations should be, will my partner upon release from prison or after extensive treatment, pose a substantial harmful threat to my family or neighbors. The statistics tend to support the conclusion that the risk is low.

Why is the recidivism rate for sex offenders low? Several factors are important:

- In most States, the post-prison treatment for sex offenders is very effective.

- Sex offender profiles are different from the profiles of criminals in general. Most sex offenders do not have a long history of criminal offenses. They are not people who are in and out of prison many times. Sex offenders are often sent to prison for long periods of incarceration after their first arrest (US Department of Justice, 2003).

- Sex offenders find prison difficult. The shame heaped on them during their incarceration is a deterrent to return to prison.

- impact on a child's life, most are horrified at what they have done. It is not the intent of this book to defend sexual offenders. It is to clarify the level of risk that your partner, if he is a sex offender, is to your family, community, and society, in general. Every child is entitled to protection against sexual abuse. In recent years, society has done a better job of educating children against improper touch and encouraging children not to keep secrets. Parents have learned to listen to what their child says rather than discount the veracity of the child. Child Protective

Service Agencies are available in many jurisdictions. States provide information on where sex offenders reside and work in their communities.

Parents also have learned that sexual offenses are perpetrated most often by adults who are trusted by the family. According to the same study by the Bureau of Justice Statistics (2003), where 9,700 sex offenders were tracked, the majority (93%) of molestations of children were committed by people who were known and trusted within or around the family.

This chapter introduced you to sex addiction from a clinical perspective. Future chapters will explore other characteristics shared by the sexually addicted, including the power of shame and the roots or origin of addiction.

It may not be possible to recreate

old dream but it is essential to formulate

new-shared dreams.

Paul Becker, LPC, Author

Chapter Three

Why Do People
Become
Sexually Addicted

Did your partner arise one day and decide he wanted to be a sex addict? Did he think through the alternatives and say to himself, "I would enjoy my life more if sex were my primary activity in life." He probably would have replied, "Of course not!" Likely, your partner did nothing to cause his sexual addiction, that is, he never consciously chose to become sexually addicted.

How did it happen? The answer to the question is important. The following are "causes" that cover how most people become sexually addicted. Try to determine which cause best describes your partner's road to sexual addiction.

Six causes of sexual addiction

Six "causes" classify the conditions underlying how people become sex addicts. The "causes," from clinical experience, address at least, 95 percent or more incidences of sex addiction. This chapter addresses female addiction in many cases, but not all.

- **Cause One –** age-inappropriate exposure to sexual behavior or material.

Four out of five adult sex addicts began their sexual behavior in childhood and carried the habit of sexual behaviors usually taught by their exposure to a childhood catalytic event into adulthood. Chapter 4 characterizes the importance of age-inappropriate exposure. It is part of a thorough discussion of the impact on children. Multiple case studies explain how sexual abuse occurs.

Causes Two and Three have a low incidence of occurrence and addressed accordingly.

- **Cause Two** – certain medications increase vulnerability to addiction.

Adderall, taken in large therapeutic doses, poses a risk of sexual addiction. For example, reported side effects to include: change in sexual ability or desire, frequent and prolonged erections (WebMD, 2017). Adderall is an amphetamine. At a therapeutic dosage, amphetamine causes emotional and cognitive effects such as euphoria and change in desire for sex.

- **Cause Three** - the consequence of significant trauma and co-existing illnesses may begin after a diagnosis of PTSD (effects of combat). Military servicemen and women can spend a significant time enduring highly stressful situations. Assigned to an unfamiliar place, in a constant state of heightened alertness, and all the while knowing they are in physical danger can lead to a desire to find some sense of relief, however fleeting it may be. For some, relief may come in the form of sexual thoughts or acts such as:

- Engaging in sexual relationships with a partner
- Having fantasies, masturbating, looking at pornography
- Other sexual behaviors (Vermillion, 2018)

Ekerns found that approximately 10 percent of civilians have an addiction to porn, while the percentage amongst military personnel is double at 20 percent (2018).

> For some, sex acts can distract the memories of the stresses and challenges military men and women face when reintegrating back into civilian society. They are looking for something to numb the bad feelings they have. Sex appears as a less dangerous alternative to using drugs or alcohol in an attempt to escape from the realities of everyday life. Sex becomes a new coping skill that potentially replaces other healthy methods of coping (Vermillion, 2018)

Unfortunately, repetitive sexual behavior leads to a habit which may result in addiction.

- **Cause Four** - for nearly two in ten sex addicts, the origin of their sexual behavior began in   late teen years or early twenties.

Illicit sex education often occurs when a sexually naive young man or woman attend school away from family or join the military. Before experiencing life away from the family, some young people lived in a sexually sterile environment. Sex was never mentioned or discussed in their homes. Parents and children were always fully clothed; sleepovers were not allowed, and, in some cases, children attended alternative schools. Children were isolated from life's normal socialization that provided an understanding of sexuality.

A sexually sterile environment creates a knowledge and experience vacuum. The vacuum implodes when the isolated teenager leaves the family environment and peers expose him/her to the world of sex. When the teenager first experienced sexual stimulation, the teen responded by going into overload, and in turn, found sexual stimulation and orgasm exceptionally pleasurable and desirable. Compulsive repetition of the pleasurable experience fosters sex addiction.

Case studies related to Cause Four

The following two case studies provide insight into the incidences of cause four.

Elijah was raised in a sexually isolated family

My parents raised us as very devout family. Protection from society's evils was activities, but because of long hours, he did not.

During my early years, I did not even know what sex meant. No discussion of bodily functions or human nature took place within the family environment. As a teenager, I did not date. The only exposure to girls was my younger sisters. One day I asked mother what the word "slut" written on the wall of a restroom meant. She dismissed my question by saying that I should not repeat bad words.

At age eighteen, I was sent off to a small, parochial college. When my dorm mates learned I never saw a pornographic magazine, they flooded me with their collections. I devoured magazines and began to masturbate daily. I felt I could not tell my parents. As time went by, my appetite for sexual material grew. I found I could not stop even when I wanted too. Finally, I talked to a clergy person about my sexual activity who helped me end my sexual behavior.

Abbott lived a confined life, which resulted in my sexual addiction

As a young child, I was frequently ill. My asthma prevented me from playing much of the year outdoors. My mother was fearful of childhood diseases carried by other children and would not invite playmates to our home. I passed the time by reading, watching television, and playing video games. I became a loner. In school, I had only a couple of friends. These friends were also interested in playing video games. I was shy and teased by several girls. I was afraid of girls and kept my distance. I did not date during high school.

During my late teen years, a new girl moved in next door. Her bedroom windows did not have drapes. Each evening, I watched her undress from my bedroom window. I used binoculars to watch and was sexually stimulated during my nightly ritual.

At age nineteen, I was arrested for peeping into windows in my neighborhood. As a form of alternative sentencing, I participated in sex offender counseling. Both men were sexually unaware during childhood. It was late in their development when they were exposed to sexual stimulation. For each, exposure to sexual material or behavior was traumatic and formed the basis of sexual addiction.

- **Cause Five** - sexual addiction can occur when there is a **lack of attachment** between the mother and child at the birth of a baby and during the early years of formation. This lack of attachment creates a **hole in the child's soul** that the adult addict tries to fill with sex.

The need for mother-child bonding is a fundamental rule of nature. A child's mother shares the attributes of attachment by actions her infant perceives as caring and provides security. For example, holding the infant, cooing while making eye contact, fondling by touching and rubbing the baby's skin/body, playing, feeding, changing the child's diaper, bathing, and other forms of contact love during the child's early formative years is part of parental attachment.

- **Cause Six - A repressive family environment** may lead a child to discover sex. Children who are introduced to sex are not always subject to aberrant behavior or material by another person.

A childhood catalytic event generally begins the process of sexual behavior, and age-inappropriate sexual stimulus is the characteristic that most often leads to a habit of sexual behavior. However, a repressive family is enough to cause a child to seek emotional comfort a family cannot provide. As such, a child can engage in self-sex or peer-to-peer behavior that is as toxic as is exposure at the hands of a perpetrator.

In a dysfunctional family, toxicity is not consistently damaging as a parent(s) who engage in repressive behavior, such as, beatings, locking a child in a confined space, physical or emotional sexual assaults. In a repressive family, a child learns to care for his/her own emotional needs to survive. The child is isolated from friends and family. Only does sexual activity provide the good feelings needed to mask conditional love and isolation.

Danny and Billy were raised in a repressive family environment

The boys were not exposed to sexual behavior by family or non-family members, nor by any other influence other than a distorted family environment. The boys began to sexually stimulate each other by rubbing their private parts together. A repressive environment is the "cause" that began their sexual encounters. A distorted family environment is an example of repression that does not provide children with the emotional nourishment they need to feel loved. Unfortunately, clinical experience suggests such child sexual behavior is not uncommon and can happen under less severe family environments.

But if anyone causes one of these little ones who believe in me to sin, it would be better for him to have a large millstone hung around his neck and to be drowned in the depths of the sea.
Matthew

Chapter Four

Exposure of a Child to Age-inappropriate Sexual Behavior or Material

This chapter explores the sexual exposure of a child. The intent is not to make you a clinical practitioner but to help you decide if your partner's sexual behavior began in childhood as it did for 81 percent of adult males.

The last chapter identified "causes" that lead to sexual addiction; this chapter begins with a presentation of the psychological characteristics that often coincide with the path to sexual addiction. While the psychological characteristics promote sexual addiction, the characteristics are not a standalone "cause." A therapy client is often aware that "something" leads him/her to therapy, but the client's understanding is limited. During therapy, a whole host of clinical factors are explored. For example, your partner is well served to identify life factors that contribute to stress, the need to act out, and the desire to overcome frustration and anxiety. "Clinical" factors are uncovered and discussed during a therapy session(s).

This chapter is composed of four parts:

- **Part One: Psychological characteristics that lead to sexual addiction**
- **Part Two: Consequences of exposure to sexual behavior or material**
- **Part Three: Children from rigid and chaotic families**
- **Part Four: Case Studies**

- **Part One: Psychological characteristics that lead to sexual addiction.**

Six characteristics, plus childhood exposure to sex, increase the disposition of a child to become a sexually-addicted adult. Primary exposure characteristics are part of this chapter. For now, the primary clinical factors related to childhood exposure to sex are:

- **Compulsion -** Inability to curtail sexual behavior. Once exposed to sex, a child is at risk to repeat the initial exposure, and repetition becomes a significant challenge for the child to stop. Compulsive behavior is a characterization of many addictions. When the sexual behavior of a child becomes repetitive, a child's ability to forego sexual behavior is weak.

- **Lack of emotional nourishment -** The father of the family is unable to provide his children with emotional nourishment. Men in therapy discuss how the lack of a nourishing emotional relationship with their father was critical to their development. While their fathers were good providers, they lacked empathy and the ability to express care and understanding. They were unable to converse with their child lovingly. A child, introduced to age-inappropriate sex, in time, may become emotionally stunted and stand a significant chance of becoming addicted as an adult.

- **Repressive family -**The child does not feel, nor is he or she valued. A repressive family is toxic to a child's development. The repressive state leads a child to seek emotional comfort that a family of origin cannot provide and may lead to child sexual activity. An addict often comes from a family environment that fails to meet the child's need for caring and affection. Children who live in repressive families feel a sense of abandonment by their parents. The parents are not present in a way that leads a child to feel confident and loved. To the contrary, a child feels isolated from parents and siblings. A repressive environment, such as that in which Danny and Billy lived, causes a child to learn to care for his or her own emotional needs to survive. As such, a child can engage in self-sex or peer-to-peer behavior that is as toxic as exposure at the hands of a perpetrator. Child sexual behavior can occur in a also occur in a dysfunctional family.

- **Abandonment** – A child experiences physical or psychological distancing, but the result is the same, that is, profound negative feelings related to the lack of love and caring. A child who is isolated feels is, why would God love me when so many better people inhabit the world?

- **Lack of attachment -** when the developmental process is ignored, an addict finds it hard to respond. Children exposed to early sex do not share what happened with their parents. An addict often tries to fill the hole in the soul with aberrant sexual behavior. The child turned adult will spend much of his/her life, searching for what their mother was unable to provide. If attachment does not take place as nature intended, children become candidates for adult sexual addiction.

- **Lack of sharing** – as stated children exposed to early sex often do not share what happened with their parents. Why do some children, exposed to early sex, not experience adult sexual addiction? If sharing what happened after a child's exposure to sex is fostered by a loving "body education program" which parents begin early in the life of the child, sex addiction will, likely, not follow. The relationship between the child and parents makes the difference. When a child shares an unwanted sexual experience with his/her parents, and a parent helps the child understand he/she is not responsible for the event and reassures the child that arousal is a normal consequence of stimulation, the child is less likely to be adversely affected. This process is called **normalization**. The relationship between the child and parent is critical in defusing the intensity of the event.

Childhood exposure to sex is a **catalytic event** and generally begins the process of addiction. Various combinations of the above lead to a habit of sexual behavior; for example, age-inappropriate sexual stimulus at a young age combined with the child's lack of sharing what happened with parents are precursors for addiction.

Matt's story of sexual objectification

Women's breasts are sexually stimulating to me. Every large breasted woman is an object for my gratification. I need a front row seat at a ball game to preclude every female within eyeshot from distracting me. Although I tried multiple interventions, I have yet to find a way to stop my objectifying female breasts.

Sexual **objectification** is treating a person as a mere object of sexual desire is a result of inadequate infantile attachment. Ferree (2010) reports, an addict who struggles with sexual behavior often struggles with the effects of abandonment as well (p. 133).

Part Two - Consequences of exposure to sexual behavior or material.

A young child exposed to sexual behavior or material will suffer consequences. A child lacks life experiences to put age-inappropriate exposure into perspective. Sexuality begins very early in life, and nature intends it to evolve with age.

For example, a child instinctively knows that pornographic material is not part of his/her normal environment. Such exposure is traumatic. For many children, the content of the sexual material will be part of a child's memory for the rest of their lives. Parents must normalize such event(s), that is, explain and put the event(s) into perspective for the child.

Most children where exposure occurred at an early age were subject to a catalytic event (Carnes, 1994). A catalytic sexual event is traumatic. Sexual exposure for them began before they understood what was happening. Developmentally, they lacked a understanding as to the consequences of engaging in sexual activity. For some, the ability to judge the morality of their sexual behavior does not occur until adulthood. Lesser but important factors co-inside with early age exposure to sex are:

- **Arousal and exposure to sex**

Arousal is the normal consequence of sexual stimulation. It is how God made us. Babies engage in self-stimulation as a normal process of self-discovery and include learning the response to touch. However, for a child, arousal is beyond the norm. Exposure to early sex can occur through self-discovery. For example, a child may discover self-stimulation and begin to repeat the stimulation and masturbation. Also, a child realizes arousal caused by another person is abnormal. A child instinctively knows the difference. The consequences are the same. When a child is first stimulated by sexual material or through the acts of self or another person, the intensity of the arousal is greater than accidental stimulation. Intense feelings dominate the child. For the first time, the brain encodes his/her sexual feelings.

Why does a child remember a catalytic event? Interestingly, it was an experience remembered with such clarity but not what the child had for dinner on his or her birthday that year; a defining moment; one the brain will remember for a lifetime.

While the child may have felt other emotions, the child's brain remembers the chemical flow, the arousal feeling. Those addicted to cocaine tell researchers that their first high on cocaine was the best they ever experience. Continued use is an attempt to recreate the first high. Likewise, without realizing it, many children try to recreate their first experience.

Furthermore, adult sexual activity frequently has similar characteristics as arousal experienced in early childhood. For example, a child introduced to pornography will seek pornography as an adult. A sexually abused child is more likely to abuse or molest children in adulthood.

- **Family environment and structure**

Sex addicts often come from a family environment that did not meet their childhood needs for affection or emotional support.

A child who feels isolated and detached from parents is unable to go to them with confidence that they will love him/her even when something bad happens. For most young children exposed to age-inappropriate behavior or material, instinct tells them that something bad has happened. The child now has a huge and troubling secret that cannot be shared. Children believe if they participate in sexual activity because they enjoy the attention or touch, they are willing participants. When children experience sexual pleasure, they are confused and may believe they are bad. Children even blame themselves for the event when all the logical signs point elsewhere. The child is often permanently damaged. Their fear discourages them from seeking the very healing that comes from parental intervention.

Isolation is a consequence of living in a family structure in which the child is not valued for being self. The child learns to withdraw to avoid humiliation or verbal abuse. When a child shares needs, feelings, dreams, and nonconforming thoughts is ridiculed or even worse, ignored, the child's psyche is damaged. The child's survival mode quickly became isolation. Perhaps some are not isolated, but they are rare. The price of isolation is loneliness. When an isolated child does not learn normal socialization skills, the consequences of childhood isolation spills over into adulthood. Interestingly, isolated people are even isolated after they marry (Becker, 2017).

- **Lack of intimacy as a causal factor for loneliness**
Carnes (2010) notes the lack of intimacy as a causal factor for loneliness:

Most sex addicts, however, come from families in which members are 'disengaged' from one another, and there is little sharing or intimacy. Children develop few skills about sharing, being vulnerable, or risking anything about themselves. As a result, they learn to trust only themselves in such families. Self-delusion is then hard to break, and secrets become more potent than reality. The worst effect is a child unable to ask for help.

To emphasize, this is the very time that a child needs a parent most. A traumatized child needs to know and feel parental love is unconditional, and a bad event does not change parental love.

- **Childhood Depressed Mood** If children believe a sexual exposure is their fault, it is easy to conclude that they will live in some level of depressed mood. Depression often follows the victim into adulthood.

- **Curse of early childhood exposure to sex**

  Introduction to aberrant sex play by a peer or older child is usually from about age five years through twelve years of age. Age-inappropriate exposure is most damaging when it occurs in early prepubescent years (Becker, 2010).

  Addict's in recovery confess to the adult realization of the consequences of childhood exposure to sexual behavior. Such realization may occur as part of spousal discovery, therapy, twelve-step program, or through the maturation process. The addict realizes one's activities are simply not fostering the lifestyle the addict now desires.

Part Three - Children from rigid or chaotic families

Carnes explains:

> The family of origin is usually either rigid or chaotic. If the family is rigid, the child believes he or she must measure up to his parents' expectations. If the child fails to meet parental expectations, the child may conclude he or she is not worthy nor deserving of their love.

> Family rules in a rigid family are conveyed explicitly, often by yelling, critical nagging, or body language. Body language in a rigid family may include a deep sigh, a frown, an abruptly disconnected conversation, or the look that could kill. The child receives the message that he or she is deficient (2010).

A rigid family is performance-based. That is, for the child to be loved, performance at the level expected by parents is made clear to the young child. Attaining good grades, success in sports, good behavior, and a physically fit body are some examples of conditional love.
The adage, children, are to be seen and not heard, is a characteristic of a rigid family. A system of rules runs the family. Parental scorn is the parent's punishment for not abiding by the family rules of behavior.

- **Sex addicts come from rigid, authoritarian families**

In his book, *Facing the Shadow*, Carnes says:

> Sex addicts also tend to come from rigid, authoritarian families. These are families in which all issues and problems are black and white. Little is negotiable, and there is only one way to do things.

Success in the family means doing what the parents want to such an extent that children give up being who they are. Normal child development does not happen. By the time children enter adolescence, they have few options. One is to become rebellious. The other is to develop a secret life about which the family knows nothing. Both positions distort reality. Both result in a distrust of authority and a poor sense of self.

If the family's rigidity is also sex-negative, sex becomes exaggerated or hidden. The forbidden may become the object of obsession. The worst-case scenario happens when the child finds one's parents do not live up to family sexual standards. For example, if the parents preach against sexual promiscuity, but if one or both have affairs, this teaches the acceptability of sexual duplicity. To pretend what is true is not true is the norm to deceive others (2010).

- **A chaotic family is on the opposite end of the spectrum**

  The chaotic family is on the opposite end of the spectrum. A child in a chaotic family thinks he has no thoughts that are his own. His parents are always penetrating the boundaries of his world. The child has no space he can call his own. In a chaotic situation, the family name is of paramount importance. It is the job of all family members to look good to the neighbors. If a member of the family fails, it was the job of the family to close ranks and protect the wounded member (Carnes, 2010).

- **The outcome from a rigid or chaotic family**

  In both a rigid and chaotic family, the child ends up feeling the same. The child believes he or she is not loved. For some, sex is considered bad or dirty. It is as if sex was a rarely discussed family secret. Such children feel isolated and seek other avenues to express themselves. A sexually abused child can experience life without ever feeling joy or love. If the family of origin was repressive or the child is a victim of parental abandonment, the child's existence is sad. Emotional needs drive everything. Sadness and the pain of not being loved are likely to trigger disturbing memories and likely negative behavior.

  Children exposed to sex early in life and raised in a repressive family learn to manage their environment for their protection. Children become fixed on survival. To a child, survival may look like turning all emotions either off or inward to avoid being hurt by the family or others. Children left to fend for themselves often grow into adulthood emotionally stunted. They may look like selfish adults who are overly attuned to getting their needs met. One need is to repeat the good feeling generated by early exposure or self-arousal.

Part Four: Case studies

Case studies are an effective means of emphasizing salient concepts and valuable illustrating tool. Case studies of early childhood exposure to sex and one study of a successful recovery now follow.

The stories allow comparison of classic exposure to sex with the stories of typical young people, some of whom were on their way to becoming addicted. Stories address various situations and environments in which the seed of sexual exposure grows into an adult addiction. Of course, multiple characteristics influence a child to continue sexual behavior.

Case studies include the characteristics generally found in the roots of sexually addicted people. They are recorded in reasonable detail to allow insight into how destructive exposure can be. A minimum of graphics and sexual detail accompanies the presentation of the stories. Those featured in the vignettes did not realize addiction may be their fate. Child sexual indoctrination may occur at a time when their human development did not allow for informed decisions. The vignettes show common themes related to the origin of sexual addiction. See if you can identify common themes.

Ann Marie's Story of Family Abuse

My family was a loving, traditional family; my father worked outside the home, and my mother raised the family. I loved them both dearly, but my Dad was the center of my universe. For a five-year-old, he walked on water. It was from this mindset that I witnessed the first shock of my young life--my beloved Dad punished my disobedient younger brother with a violent spanking. I was terrified, tried to stop it, and vowed to never commit anything "bad" for fear of being punished in that manner.

The trauma of this event was compounded a year later when I was caught talking in class by my first-grade teacher. In response to her questioning and in fear of "being bad," I denied it. In front of all my classmates, she firmly slapped me right across the face. It was so unexpected that I wet my pants. I was horrified, humiliated, and ashamed. That afternoon, I told my Mom what had happened but was too scared to tell my father. I crawled into a growing habit of doing whatever was necessary to be loved and accepted. If that meant shutting my mouth, going along, being in the background, so be it. I was creating a haven for myself - or trying to do so.

A year later, a close male member of our extended family sexually abused me. I trusted and admired him and his touching me "in that way" drove me into angst. Why would he do this? I felt alone and confused. Still afraid of losing my father's love (and being punished), I confided the abuse to my mother who, once again, did nothing to interfere or protect me. But I won't ever forget the shock and the feeling of disgust with my own body and eventually my sexuality. The compilation of these events led me to become bulimic, an illness I fought for decades. During the remaining years of my childhood and even throughout college, I continued to live on hyper-alert for who could turn on me and hurt me, I shied away from attention, participation and avoided conflict at all costs. The shame and humiliation I felt from my earlier experiences returned to haunt me. Anger and disapproval would trigger me to shut down. I believed the adults in my life were not worthy of my trust and could betray me at a moment's notice. The pain wasn't just emotional-I felt it physically as a million tiny pinpricks in a voodoo doll.

Nate's Story of Family Sexual Abuse

From my earliest memory, I recall my Mother tying me to a chair when I got in her way, which was often. She constantly yelled at me--telling me I could do better. Satisfying my mother's expectations was impossible. She was a perfectionist.

My Father was not around much. He worked away from home for months at a time. When he was home, he did not have time for my brother or me. I have no memory of a pleasant conversation with Dad. I do not remember him teaching me anything meaningful about sports or life in general. What I remember was his collection of pornographic magazines. Around age ten, I found his collection and wondered why he kept them.

What impressed me about the pornographic magazines were women with large breasts. When I stared at the pictures, I felt strange, what I now know as arousal. My Mother also had large breasts. My arousal feelings turned to shame. I remember scanning the daily newspapers in search of images of women with large breasts. As a teenager, I would ogle my Dad's magazines and fantasize about having sex with the women.

Nate has a very vivid memory of an encounter with his father. Around age twelve, he remembers his enraged father strip him naked in front of their home and beat him. Other children, including neighborhood girls, watched. Nate remembers a profound sense of humiliation and shame. Later he sought out one of the girls who watched to engage her in sexual activity. He felt hatred for her and his father.

Polly's story of Sexual Abuse by an Older Boy

Polly is a vivacious seven-year-old girl. She never met a person who she did not like. She is popular with the other children who live on her street, particularly Mike. Mike pays attention to her and gives her candy. One day, much to Polly's surprise, Mike kissed her.

Well, they were friends, and Mike is good for her. She reasoned a kiss was OK. However, Mike talked to her about things that made her uncomfortable. He asked if she wanted to touch his private parts. Since she did not have any brothers, she was curious but was reluctant to say yes. Sometime later, Mike asked Polly if she wanted to see the shack the boys on the block built. Polly again was curious, as she knew the boy's shack is off-limits to the girls on the street. She gleefully said she would like to see it.

They were all alone in the shack, and Mike told her not to be afraid. He asked her to stand up. Mike reached up under her dress and pulled down her underpants. Polly was confused. What was Mike going to do next? Mike exposed himself and asked Polly if she would touch him. She screamed, "no." She panicked. She wanted Mike to get off her, and she screamed again. Her screaming scared Mike, and he ran away.

Polly and her mother held no secrets, and Polly told her mother what happened. Mike is forbidden to play with the children on the street and is in therapy. Fortunately, Polly's mother was able to sooth Polly by telling her Mike's assault was not her fault. Her mother normalized the event for Polly. Hopefully, because of her mother's ability to normalize what happened, the event will become only a vague memory for Polly.

Simon's story of Sexual Abuse by Older Girls

Around age five, Simon played unattended with neighborhood children up and down the street. Late one summer afternoon, two older neighborhood girls took him to one of the girl's back yards and made a tent with blankets. Once inside the tent, the girls wanted to play doctor, and Simon would be their patient. They removed his underwear and tickled him. He felt very uncomfortable and confused when they touched him.

It was then his turn and they bared their bottoms. He was surprised. Their bottoms looked nothing like his. In therapy, he said he felt cheated. (laugh)

Time passed quickly, and Simon realized he was late for dinner. He was supposed to be home before the six o'clock fire whistle sounded. Upon hearing the whistle blow, he ran home. When he entered his home, his clothes were in disarray. His shirt was out, his pants unbuttoned, and he was missing a sock. He felt frightened and was sure Mother would question his state of undress. He wanted to tell his mother what the girls had done with him. Instead, his mother yelled at him for not being properly dressed. Why didn't his mother ask him why his clothes were in such disarray? Did she know what he had been doing? He felt very confused.

Several weeks later, one of the older girls returned and took Simon into the woods across from where he lived. This time there were no blankets to hide under. A neighborhood child told Simon's father what was going on in the woods. Simon's father shamed him. Simon felt that he was a very bad boy. His interest in sex play with neighborhood children grew. He wondered what was wrong with him.

Jimmy's Story of Sexual Abuse by an Adult

Jimmy was an affable boy around the age of ten. Both of Jimmy's parents were involved in their professions. Jimmy's father was a workaholic lawyer. Jimmy's mother was a full-time professor at a local college. The family belonged to a prestigious country club with all the amenities of golf, tennis, swimming, and social events. Jimmy's parents worked during the day. During the summer, they dropped Jimmy off at the country club on their way to work.

At the county club, Jimmy's schedule was complete with lessons. Early in the morning, he had a golf lesson followed by practice on the driving range. Early afternoon he had a tennis lesson. Often on the days when a tennis match did not follow his lesson, he would go swimming with other boys like himself.

Jimmy liked tennis because, as he understood later as an adult, Steve, the tennis pro, paid a lot of attention to him. Jimmy took to spending afternoon hours in the tennis shack with Steve. Steve taught him how to re-string a racket and other useful skills. One day while spending time with Steve, Jimmy said that he wanted to join his friends at the pool. However, that day, Jimmy forgot to bring his swim trunks. Steve said he had a pair of swim trunks in the lost and found that probably would fit Jimmy. He suggested Jimmy try on the trunks at the tennis shack to see if they fit him. As he changed, Steve asked Jimmy if he played with his "willy." Steve asked him to show him how he did it. Jimmy did not want to disappoint his friend Steve.

As the summer went on, Steve found more opportunities to initiate sexual stimulation with Jimmy. He introduced Jimmy to pornography. Jimmy liked the attention Steve showed to him and felt that perhaps their secret behavior was Steve's way of showing him how to be a man, at least that was what Steve said.

Jimmy never shared his behavior with his parents. A time when his parents were open to listening just never happened. Jimmy knew something was wrong with his need to frequently act out. He was confused over the conflict between the good feelings he experienced, and the secrets Steve made him keep. He did not know the consequences of continuing his behavior...how could he?

After the summer, Jimmy and Steve no longer saw each other. Steve moved to a warmer climate. Jimmy continued to masturbate whenever he felt he wanted to repeat the good feelings he first experienced with Steve.

Jimmy entered therapy in his early thirties to deal with compulsive self-stimulation and pornography. Jimmy was committed to shedding his victimhood. His recovery journey took several years and was successful.

Aaron's Story of Sexual Addiction Passed Down from His Father.
Aaron entered therapy to address sexual behaviors that he found disturbing. Besides, he wanted help to deal with a rather large collection of paper pornography he inherited from his father.

Aaron told his story:

I thought I grew up in a normal family, but perhaps it was not so normal after all. I now know it seemed normal because I had nothing with which to compare my family. I had a stay-at-home mom and a father who was a supervisor at a local sheet metal plant. My brother, Jacob, was seven years older, and my sister, Rebecca, was two years younger.

My father craved his privacy. He would arrive home at 6:00 in the evening and mother had dinner on the table as he walked in the door. My parents insisted each of us talk about what happened at school. If we were critical of a teacher, my father would declare the teacher correct even without knowing all the facts. My mother never crossed my father but often complained about him to us children when he was not around. I never remember mom and dad being affectionate to each other in front of the children.

After dinner, my father took his newspaper and went to his study. Once he entered his study, he closed the door and, for the rest of the evening, he was not to be disturbed behind his closed door.

One winter day, I came down with a bad cold, and mother made me stay home from school. She had some a doctor's appointment that day and told me to rest on the couch in the living room while she was gone. She said she would return in a few hours.

For a ten-year-old boy, resting on the couch does not last very long, even if he has a bad cold. I started thinking about what was behind dad's closed the door. I knew I was forbidden to go into his room, but my curiosity got the best of me. With trepidation, I opened the door and peered in. On the other wall was a large closet. I knew I should not open, but I did. Dad had constructed shelves in the closet. On the shelves from floor to ceiling were stacks of magazines. Since I had gone this far, I was curious about what kind of magazine my dad found interesting. The first magazine I opened had a foldout page in the middle with a picture of a woman without clothes that showed her private parts. I was disturbed by the picture but fascinated. I remember my first thought was, why a woman would allow someone to take a picture of her bottom? As I looked through several other magazines, I was surprised by my feelings. It seemed as if fireworks were going off in my head, and even more surprising; I had an erection. I was totally confused and scared. I simply did not understand.

After dinner that evening, my father went to his study. After a few minutes, my father stormed into the living room and, in a rage, began to yell at me. He knew I had stayed home from school, and my mother was not home part of the day. Much of what he yelled seemed strange, but it was clear he knew I had entered his closet. He called my brother and sister into the room and pulled off all my clothes. He yelled something like, 'you want sex; I'll give it to you.' He proceeded to beat me until I felt welts on my bottom. I as so embarrassed that my sister saw me naked. I was even more ashamed when my brother began laughing at me. I wondered how I could have done such an evil thing.

I never entered dad's room again while he was alive. I do not think I was ever quite the same after that day. The next day my mother opened the Bible and read to me the passage from Genesis about the fall of Adam and Eve in the garden. I remember thinking I must be as evil as Adam and Eve. How could anyone ever love me?

During therapy, Aaron was encouraged to talk to his brother about what it was like for him to grow up in his family. Aaron thought he was the only black sheep in the family. Aaron was grateful to learn that his experience in his dad's room and his beating were also experienced by his brother several years before. Jacob told him he had laughed out of embarrassment during Aaron's ordeal. Aaron learned that pornography and masturbation were serious problems for Jacob as well. Aaron learned many things about his family from Jacob. Both needed to explore generational sexual behavior. They realized their grandfather, father, and they were sexually addicted. Both Aaron and Jacob had young children. They pledged to stop passing the family curse on from generation to generation.

Aaron and Jacob continued in therapy together. Both addressed the sexual behavior they carried from childhood into adulthood. The brothers also opened a dialogue with their sister, Rebecca, and found that she, too, had been damaged by the family environment. The siblings are now close and are joyful that they addressed the "baked cake" of addiction handed down to them from previous generations.

Patrick's Story of a Babysitter's Sexual Abuse.

Patrick recalls his introduction to sexual behavior when he was around eight-years-old. A cousin frequently slept over at his house. One evening she was assigned to babysit him. Patrick did not feel it was particularly strange that she wanted to bath him. On the other hand, he remembers, during the bath, she initiated sex play. After the bath, she crawled into his bed with him without PJ's. He said he did not remember feeling that way before. However, he knew for us to go to bed together would not have occurred if his parents had been home. He remembers wondering why his cousin chose him.

He remembers very clearly his cousin telling him that if he told anyone about what happened, she would blame it all on him. She told him he was a bad boy for having an erection. This made Patrick even more confused. How could such good feelings be wrong and entirely his fault? He agreed with his cousin. He indeed was a bad boy. He also agreed if he told his parents he would be punished. His cousin abused Patrick several more times during his prepubescent years.

Bill's Success Story

Bill said:

Whenever I see a scantily-dressed woman, I am into my fantasy just she and me. I have enjoyed my fantasies for so long, how could I give them up? While I tell myself, I don't want to act out, I have grown to like how it makes me feel.

Bill also saw what it was doing to him.

Acting out is the most dishonest thing I do. I want my wife and friends to see me as a good person, but if they knew my secret, well, so much for the good person. When am I going to beat this? When am I going to become the person I want to be? When am I going to put my wife and not my fantasies, first? I have got to try.

In counseling, Bill learned, the moment of choice is the instant he becomes aware a fantasy has begun. It begins before Bill has a choice, but once aware, he can ask himself, "Do I want to go there?" Bill decided to try sounding his awareness alarm by changing how he viewed scantily-clad women. He began to say to himself that person could be my sister. It helped, but he found he did not fully drop the image. He stored the images in his brain's file cabinet and brought them out as he lay in bed, waiting for sleep to come.

Bill talked about his commitment.

> I delay gratification, but I don't seem to be committed to doing away with it. I want to do better. I am sick and tired of the pain. I am sick of being sick.

Bill went back to the drawing board and mapped out a different approach to his awareness alarm. He began individual therapy with a competent sex addiction therapist, attended a Twelve-step program, and found an accountability partner at his church who struggled with alcohol as a younger man. He talked about his wife. He said he loved her and thought he did not have the right to put fantasizing about other women ahead of his relationship with her. He first dealt with his secrets. With the help of his therapist, Bill shared his secret life with his wife. His wife was shocked and hurt, but with time she understood the courage, it took Bill to share his shame--his secrets. She understood his desire to commit to putting her first.

Bill talked about his approach.

I want to commit. I want to stop the pain. To put my fantasies first, myself first, is acting like a selfish child. I do not have a right to do that; it is not fair to Susan or our children. I am going to adopt a new mantra. When a visual sexual image tempts me, I will invoke my awareness alarm, and I will say to myself, I do not have the right to go there.

Bill found that it was not an easy commitment. He had been in the habit of entertaining sexual images for a long time. With time, and with the help of his counselor, Twelve-step group, and accountability partner, Bill surrendered himself and began to experience repeated success. He worked on becoming aware of the inception of a fantasy and began to exercise his choice; I do not have the right to go there. He used alternative healthy fantasies, prayer, and other techniques to clear his mind of sexual thoughts.

After about eight months.

> I wondered if I could defeat my addiction. It had been part of my life since I was a wet-behind-the-ears kid. My fantasies and self-stimulation are where I went to deal with my pain. I know that now.

An interesting thing happened a few days ago. Do you know the park on 8th Street? As I was driving by, a couple of young women were lying out in the sun, and of course, they had much flesh exposed. In the past, this would have been more than I could have--you know what I mean. This time, my mantra came into my head, 'I do not have the right to go there.' I found it easy to leave the girls (someone's daughters) in the park.

I think that it is becoming impossible for me 'to go there.' After having invested eight months of changing my response to environmental temptation, I would be so disappointed in myself if I went back to my old ways. Going back is no longer an option.

Bill found strong reasons for changing his behavior, and he used techniques to help clear his mind of offending thoughts. The techniques, by themselves, will not make the difference.

However, strong commitment, along with using techniques, made the difference for Bill.

What did Bill do to help himself?

- Found that acting out was causing more pain than pleasure
- Found reasons to change his behavior, that is, his relationship with himself, friends, and most important, Susan, his wife
- Chose a sex addiction therapist to help him expose his secrets to the light of day
- Joined a Twelve-step program
- Asked an accountability partner to help him
- Made a high-level commitment to himself and his loved ones to change his behavior
- Used a mantra when he came across environmental temptation. "I do not have the right to go there."
- Began to see women, not as objects, but as people, someone's mother, daughter, etc., and worked at his commitment day-by-day until it became part of him.

As time went by, Bill and Susan found that their marriage, while better, still had weaknesses. A therapist helped them to understand that they had a codependent relationship. Family therapy helped the family to understand the roles each played and how codependency was toxic to Bill's recovery from addiction. His therapist also taught Bill to change his lifestyle. He programmed in more healthy activities, made new friends, and became closer to his God.

Review of the Concepts Found in the Vignettes

It is critical to understand that your man did not make a conscious choice to introduce aberrant sexual behavior into his childhood. Your partner was once a victim, as you are today. However, he cannot remain a victim. Society and religious mores call him to accept and repair what went wrong, that is, reject living his adult life in the pits of sexual degradation. He is called to begin a recovery journey.

During the recovery journey, he will have the opportunity to heal and look forward to an addiction-free life.

Your feelings and reaction to your partner's acting-out behavior may also be conditioned upon your childhood, teen, or experiences in adult years. A man and a woman often give off unconscious symbiotic signals. In discussions with couples where the man is addicted, women often disclose they experienced some form of physical, emotional, or sexual abuse during their earlier life. Your reaction to your partner's condition may also be a reaction to how you were hurt. This subject will be discussed further in Chapter 6 on codependency.

In this section, you are asked to think about the vignettes just presented and identify when the following characteristics were demonstrated.

- **Characteristic: Experience of a catalytic event.**

Each of the vignettes demonstrates how exposure to age-inappropriate material or behavior is the catalytic event upon which adult sexual addiction is formed. Not all readily remember their catalytic event. Sexual exploitation of a child is a traumatic event—the memory of which is often repressed. It is a natural defense for some children who experience a traumatic event to detach mentally in the present moment.

Some do not connect the actions of parents or relatives with sexual abuse. For example, Lewis was bathed by his mother, who included hand washing of his genitals until age twelve. Lewis came to be counseled to address compulsive masturbation without the use of pornography. It took Lewis several months before he connected his mother's actions with his propensity to masturbate. When Lewis realized the connection, he was horrified because he had begun to repeat the same behavior with his young son. It was not on his radar screen that the actions of his mother could be at the root of his addiction.

Some do not connect the actions of parents or relatives with sexual abuse. For example, Lewis was bathed by his mother, who included hand washing of his genitals until age twelve. Lewis came to be counseled to address compulsive masturbation without the use of pornography. It took Lewis several months before he connected his mother's actions with his propensity to masturbate. When Lewis realized the connection, he was horrified because he had begun to repeat the same behavior with his young son. It was not on his radar screen that the actions of his mother could be at the root of his addiction.

It may be difficult for your partner to share his catalytic event with you. It is often difficult for a man to share his experiences with a trained therapist, let alone with someone, he fears may leave him. It is good advice to wait until your partner has been in therapy for several months before you ask him to share his secrets and, in many cases, the source of his profound shame. The best place to disclose secrets is in joint therapy because the therapist is trained to explain how your partner's behavior fits into a larger picture of life.

- **Characteristic: Exposure to age-inappropriate material or behavior.**

A child's experiences may be embarrassing. Being caught taking his sister's candy after Halloween may be embarrassing, but it will not have a lasting effect. Being sent to the principal's office for talking in class is not a lasting traumatic event. Yet, children exposed to sexual events experience consequences. Such events are age-inappropriate.

- **Characteristic: Experience of arousal.**

God made humans to experience sexual arousal. God did not make children to experience sexual arousal at the pleasure of an adult or another person more mature in his or her sexual experience or understanding. In therapy, a man reported that the feeling of arousal he experienced during his catalytic event was greater in intensity than any arousal since that time. The cocaine addict experiences his greatest high the first time he is introduced to cocaine. Some cocaine addicts say they spend the rest of their life chasing that high. Since the high experienced by the child during his catalytic event is so powerful, it is not difficult to understand why he would seek to repeat the pleasurable feelings.

Carnes found that 81 percent of addicts he surveyed remember being abused sexually in some way as a child. The abuse may have been blatant or subtle. If your partner was exposed to age-inappropriate sexual activity or sexually explicit material, it might have created a lasting memory and desire to repeat the same behavior or a derivative of that behavior in adult life. The very fact that he can recall such age-inappropriate sexual activity or sexually explicit material affirms that it did affect him (1992).

For many sexually abused children, life presents other psychological problems in addition to abuse. For these children, repeating the pleasurable experience of arousal becomes a way of self-medicating feelings of lack of attachment and family abandonment, low self-worth, and lack of love in their life. The repetition of the arousal behavior also becomes habitual, and thus the root of adult addiction.

- **Characteristic: Experience feelings of shame**.

  Shame and addiction go together and are often passed down from one generation to the next. Physical, emotional, and sexually abused children often come from shame-based families. Shame binds a man to addiction.

- **Characteristic: Experience feelings of shame and guilt.**

  While shame and guilt go together they are different. Guilt knows a person has violated one's standards, that is, a reaction to having done something regrettable. Shame involves knowing the person has have done something others would find reprehensible. Guilt is a positive reminder. Shame goes to the core judgment of self—flawed. Guilt may help a man choose to deal with his aberrant sexual behavior, but shame keeps him addicted.

  In another sense shame and guilt are not the same. A guilty child knows he or she has done something wrong. Feelings of guilt emanate from the child's conscience. An ashamed child feels something is wrong with him/her.

  John Bradshaw (1988) states,

  > Guilt says I've made a mistake; shame says I am a mistake.
  > Guilt says what I did was not good; shame says I am no
  > good. It makes a profound difference.
  >> Shame is a destructive feeling. It contributes to a sense
  >> of sadness and depressed mood. Acting out is a form of

self-medication which makes the addict feel better. Unfortunately, more shame and the cycle begins again. Addiction and obsessive disorders are symptoms of being abandoned and shamed in childhood, according to Bradshaw (1988).

A child knows one's feelings are different after arousal. He or she knows the behavior generally occurs in a secretive environment, and the child is told not to tell. The child may know it was wrong and may feel guilty but, more importantly, the child's mind is programmed to feel that he or she is bad, that something is terribly wrong. Improper sexual events ignite a child's sense of shame, so much so, that the feeling of shame, 'I am defective,' often stays with the child for many years to come.

It is normal for a child to think he or she is at fault when something bad happens. For example, when the parents' divorce, it is common for a therapist to hear a child says, "if only I had been a better boy or girl, Mom and Dad would not have separated." The same cross-wired thinking occurs when the child is a victim of improper sexual events. The child assumes he or she is at fault.

- **Characteristic: Living in a non-nourishing family environment and structure.**

Most of the males portrayed in the vignettes throughout this book were psychologically damaged by growing up in a dysfunctional family. The families of origin were unable to provide the emotional nourishment the children needed for healthy development.

While many did not have a strong relationship with their mothers, the lack of paternal support is particularly toxic. From a societal perspective, fathers are viewed as normal if they provide housing, schooling, food, clothing, and other necessities. They may even attend some of the child's school or sporting events. However, invariably, something is missing from the relationship between a child and his father. The child did not have a healthily bond with his father in just about every case where the child becomes an addicted adult.. There are many reasons why the father was unable to bond with his child. The most common of which is the father did not have a positive role model for teaching how to treat his child. Also, alcohol, compulsive work habits, drugs, and even sex may cause a barrier to healthy family relationships. The bottom line, conversely, is children with loving and supportive fathers rarely become addicted.

In a small percentage, sexual addiction came from another source. For example, Post-Traumatic Stress Disorder (PTSD) may cause significant anxiety and depression. Addictive behavior may follow. Besides, psychiatric disorders, including manic-depressive conditions, schizophrenia, personality disorders, and substance dependence, can be the source of sexual addiction.

Why Can't the Addict Just Stop His Aberrant Sexual Behavior?

Your partner likely promised many times to stop his aberrant sexual behavior. He probably stopped for short periods, but invariably he gave in to sexual urges and returned to old habits. The rest of this chapter addresses the multiple factors that keep those sexually addicted attached to their aberrant sexual behavior.

Multiple reasons hold one captive to addictive behavior, including but not limited to:

- Lack of a moral compass.

- Habit.

- Some brain functions and chemicals foster addiction.

- Continued use of sexual thinking and fantasies keep the addiction alive.

- **Behaviors repeated in adulthood**

Are behaviors once witnessed or performed as a child repeated as an adult? Even if a child despised the behavior, he or she may repeat the behavior and may continue to do so into adulthood. As such, childhood sexual behavior becomes adult sexual behavior. For example, early childhood attachment to pornography is often repeated in adulthood. Abused children may abuse as adults. Children exposed to adulterous parental affairs may do likewise as adults. A high percent of addicts come from families where other addictions were present. If you are looking for the link to the type of behavior giving your partner difficulty today, look back to his childhood. You are likely to find the trail.
The stories from this Chapter focus on common family environments and early childhood exposure to age-inappropriate sexual stimulation. For some, the life-changing event occurred later in life or not all. The late occurrence can be the result of a sheltered childhood, rape, or coming-out of severe depression as a teen or adult. Adult onset of sexual addiction can result from medication or trauma.

Our sickness is between our ears

Source Unknown

Chapter Five

Sexual Addiction
Curse—Shame

The man and his wife were both naked, and they felt no shame (Genesis 2:25).

Scripture tells us that God's vision of humanity did not include sexual shame. Adam and Eve before the fall did not see their bodies as objects of desire, but simply part of their loving relationship. After the fall, Adam and Eve were subject to shame.

The LORD God made garments of skin for Adam and his wife and clothed them (Genesis 3:21).

Therefore, shame began for all humanity to experience. Shame can be a positive attribute—a self-regulating emotion. A sense of shame tells us that our actions or behaviors do not meet personal or societal standards of acceptability. Humanity uses shame as a restraint against offending others. Shame is part of our conscience. Without a strong and morally correct conscience, society would degenerate into chaos. In general, then, a sense of shame is beneficial.

A nearly universal trait of those sexually addicted is a profound sense of shame. For an addicted man, shame is not a self-regulating emotion. Shame trumps the addict's sense of being, his sense of self-worth, and his judgment of whether he is an acceptable member of society. His shame binds him to negative thinking and self-loathing. Not only does he view the world through his shame, but he also becomes shame. He sees himself as unable to control his appetites; that is, he is unable to manage his thinking and fantasies and unable to regulate his compulsive need to repeat sexual behavior. He experiences shame as "embarrassment, dishonor, disgrace, inadequacy, humiliation, or chagrin" (Broucek, 1991).

- **Shame and relationships**

For the most part, a sexually addicted man's relationships are filtered through his sense of shame. For example, he is often attracted to a woman who he believes is morally superior. In contrast, his sense of shame tells him he is morally deficient. His sense of shame tells him that associating with a morally superior partner may help him overcome his sexual addiction. Paradoxically, he establishes an unbalanced relationship. He perceives himself as the naughty boy who gives his partner the power to punish and admonish him. Contrary to expectations, when the man lives in an inferior ego position, he permits himself to behave like a naughty child who sexually acts out. This syndrome is called codependency, and Chapter 8 provides a comprehensive discussion of co-dependency where the male is sexually addicted.

Shame serves to distance family members from each other. Shame is often the product of abandonment for children in a dysfunctional family. The father and mother are simply not there for their children. The impact of shame often begins before the child has a sense of relationship. Even a pre-verbal child in a shame-based family can sense the lack of emotional warmth—reflective of shame. The most toxic effect of shame is a distancing between the father and the son—the son who will become addicted.

Bradshaw (2005) says:

> When children have shame-based parents, they identify with them. This is the first step in a child's internalizing shame. Trauma allows 'shame thinking' to blossom from deep roots in culture, religion, family, or our childhood past. As children, we tend to blame ourselves for things that happen around us, because we are limited in our capacity to think about others being responsible. In a five-year-old's mind if something bad happened, then she or he must have deserved it. Therefore, the universe makes sense (Panes).

> In general, all addicts are subject to the impact of shame. As such, shame is associated with addiction regardless of the type of addiction.

- **Generational shame**
  Shame is multi-generational. An addicted man often comes from a

family with a history of addiction and thus shame. It is common for an addicted man to have a father who was, or is, addicted to one or more weaknesses, including alcohol, drugs, gambling, eating, work, and frequent sex. For a man who abuses children, it is also common to learn that one or both father's parents suffered abuse as children. Thus, abuse is often multi-generational in the life of the family of origin.

- **Shame and the man**

A man who feels he is flawed usually does not share his innermost feelings. Picture this: John approaches guests at a party and says,

> "Hi, my name is John. I have a habit that I want to share with you. I love to go on the Internet and look for women who have (in detail). Once I find images that stimulate my libido, I begin a perverse ritual of acting out by (in detail)."

It just does not happen. Moreover, if it did, John would not be invited back to the party or any other social engagement. John may have difficulty sharing the details of his behavior with any other person, including a therapist. His profound sense of shame keeps his private world behind a mask of respectability. Guests at the party would be more likely to hear about John's involvement with his church, boy scouts, or business pursuits, but not about his acting-out behavior.

As you read John's vignette, did you feel a sense of shame? Were you happy that the details were not disclosed? Would you feel more shame if

John revealed, in detail, how he achieved orgasm? Sexual shame in the United States is pervasive. For the sexually addicted man, shame is compounded. He deals with his own sense of self-disgust as well as family shame.

John Bradshaw (2005) describes the impact of shame on the man:

Finally, when shame has been completely internalized, nothing about you is okay. You feel flawed and inferior; you have the sense of being a failure. There is no way you can share your inner self because you are an object of contempt to yourself. When you are contemptible to yourself, you are no longer in you. To feel shame is to feel seen in an exposed and diminished way. When you are an object to yourself, you turn your eyes inward, watching and scrutinizing every minute detail of behavior. This internal critical observation is excruciating. It generates a tormenting self-consciousness. This paralyzing internal monitoring causes withdrawal, passivity, and inaction.

- **Shame and recovery**

    If shame rules the life of an addicted man, recovery is slow and torturous. Until the man begins to look shame in the eye—by facing his secrets and the lies he tells to permit himself to act out, recovery will be an illusion. Rarely can he acknowledge shame without the help of his family, friend, pastor, or therapist? Since a shame-based man is his object of contempt, the last thing he needs is condemning words and more shame from his family. As a man contemplates recovery, he needs support not more shame.

Seth and Janet Overcome Shame by Disclosure.

Seth has been in and out of sexual addiction therapy for years. He has not been sexually sober for more than a week or two at a time. Seth works out of his home several days a week. Once his spouse and children leave for work or school in the morning, Seth's temptation becomes powerful. Seth frequently bends to temptation. After fighting temptation for a while, Seth will go onto the Internet, to search for erotic images and subsequently masturbate. If Seth leaves home early in the morning and heads to the library or Starbucks to use their Wi-Fi to do his work, he does not act out.

During group therapy, Seth revealed the nature of his Internet images of choice. Seth seeks out transvestites and sexual behavior. Seth remembered several incidents when he was eight-years-old. He and his sister would go into their mother's bedroom and put on her clothing. Seth found his mother's underwear comforting. Seth characterized his mother as distant and not very affectionate. The therapist hypothesized that Seth found dressing in his mother's underwear was a way of obtaining a sense of attachment he craved to have with her. Seth was not looking for a sexual connection to his mother, but simply normal emotional nourishment. Seth quickly saw the link between what happened in childhood and his adult acting-out behavior. He realized he continued to fill the hole in his soul by repeating similar behavior he experienced as a child.

Seth and his therapist talked about how he could make an adult choice to seek legitimate intimacy rather than act out. He noted while he and his wife had marital relations, he did not feel a sense of intimacy with his wife. He speculated if he had an intimate relationship with his wife; the dynamics of his cravings would possibly change.

The therapist suggested to Seth that he disclose his story to Janet. His immediate reaction was he could not do so. He was fearful that Janet would reject him and possibly leave him. However, after more talk, he agreed to disclose his behavior. Janet was open to marital intimacy. She too craved intimacy from her husband.

- **Shame and trauma**

It is common for a woman who has experienced physical, emotional, or sexual trauma to be fearful of engaging in marital sex. She does not feel safe; she no longer trusts men.

Wendy Malts (2001) says it this way:

> The abuse shaped the way I came to think about myself sexually. Because I had experienced strong sexual feelings prematurely, in a situation clouded by fear, and without anyone to help me make sense of the experience, I concluded as a child that there must be something terribly wrong with *me.*

Frequently, trauma and shame affect both partners where addiction resides. As such, both partners benefit from counseling. Both partners and the marriage are strengthened as each does their own work.

**If one causes one of these little ones
who believe in me to sin,
it would be better for him to have a
large millstone hung
around his neck and to be drowned
in the depths of the sea.**

Matthew 18:6

Chapter Six

The Roots of Sexual Addiction

Addict's ask, "Why did I become sexually addicted? Why did I become a sex addict? What did I do to cause my addiction? What could I have done differently?" How did it happen? While the answer to the question is important and may diminish one's shame, nevertheless, he still needs to make life changes to set the stage for recovery.

Because the child did not confide in his parents as to what happened sexually, the child lives in a secret state of isolation and dysfunction. Since he did not disclose his sexual activities to any adult, the child lacks a "moral compass" to inform him of the effigy of his behavior and its consequences. Likely, he will face life as a sex addict unless some form of intervention provides him with insight. The light from the moral compass often does not come on until mid-adulthood. I contend that strict moral responsibility begins when the addict discovers his moral compass. A moral compass is often introduced into the life of the addict when his aberrant sexual behaviors are discovered, or some form of interdiction challenges his addictive behavior. Until that time, the addict "knows," "but doesn't know." This is one of the complexities of sexual addiction, and it is hard to accept.

Habit

Multi-tasking is a byword in our society. The news media show clips of people talking on cell phones while driving, eating while driving, and even reading the newspaper or a book while driving. Why do people think they can do at least two things at once? Multi-tasking drivers believe that their driving skill has become so indoctrinated into their brains that they no longer need to think about responses to road situations.

Sexual acting out is not like driving a car on the interstate, but the call to act out has been similarly indoctrinated into the brain. Perhaps an applicable word is a habit. People rely on habit-based skills to drive vehicles, and sex addicts repeat behavior partially out of habit.

Altering the brain

The brain is the center of addiction. The brain determines what is pleasurable and what is not. The pleasure from normal activities, such as, reading a book, eating an ice cream cone, taking a walk, or going to a movie do not lead to addiction. Each of these activities is pleasurable, but the intensity is not sufficient to program the brain to foster compulsive repeating of the behavior.

However, the pleasure from sexual activity, as intended by nature, is highly enjoyable. It is one way that nature helps humanity to perpetuate itself. During sexual activity, the brain's chemicals tell it, "That was so pleasurable; I would like to do it again." The brain remembers that message and encourages the addict to repeat the sexual activity to generate pleasurable feelings. When this happens repeatedly, particularly when it begins in youth, the brain's neurotransmitters become very sensitive to the need for sexual stimulation. The brain repeatedly calls for a renewed flow of pleasurable chemical activity. The brain is altered; it now considers repetitive sexual stimulation normal.

When orgasm occurs, the brain is charged with endorphins. It records the experience as a euphoric moment; "Wow, that was enjoyable." Some runners talk about a runner's high, an experience they like to repeat. An orgasm causes a significant "rush;" an experience addicts like to repeat.

Do you wonder why the feeling during an orgasm does not last? The simplistic answer is that when endorphins are used up, so is the euphoric feeling. This explains why a man no longer feels romantic after he has achieved a climax. The normal state of the brain is altered during the buildup and orgasm.

The chemical flow of endorphins overrides feelings of low mood and even pain. It is the combination of the reduction in pain and the feeling of euphoria that makes acting out sexually such a powerful experience, one that becomes compulsive for the addict.

Brain chemicals

Brain chemicals are at the root of acting-out behavior. It is enlightening to understand how important brain chemicals foster arousal and organism and inhibit the addict's desire to end his addictive behavior. The following is a synopsis of how seven classes of brain chemicals function. They cause the brain to crave chronic viewing of pornography and engaging in masturbation.

- **Testosterone.**

Testosterone is a steroid hormone that is responsible for the development and maintenance of masculine characteristics such as deepening of the voice, muscle growth, facial and body hair, and penis size. Testosterone in the adult also relates to social behaviors. For example, social experiences such as competition cause testosterone levels to rise or fall.

Testosterone flows into the bloodstream in response to sexual stimulation; that is, it prepares the body and brain for sexual intimacy. External stimulus (pornography) or internal stimulus (sexual fantasy or a memory of a sexual encounter) increase the flow of testosterone and raise sexual desire. (Struthers, 2009, p. 100). When the stimulus is chronic (frequent exposure to pornography), the heightened sexual desire takes the brain to a higher level of craving for sexual activity, and any signal is a trigger to act out.

A man in a healthy marriage has a lower level of testosterone and thus is less prone to react to sexual temptation outside the marriage—providing he has not been living a dual sexual life (Burnham et al.,

2003). Paradoxically, irritability and anger are promoted by low testosterone.

- **Dopamine.**

Dopamine is a neurotransmitter, that is, a chemical released by nerve cells that sends signals to other nerve cells. It regulates the brain's *reward and pleasure center*. Dopamine enables the human to perceive a reward and to act to move toward sexual intimacy. For example, dopamine triggers feelings of ecstasy, exhilaration, sexy mood, and a craving for sexual intimacy (Kastleman, 2007, p. 40).

Dopamine involves many different neuropathways. Marital relations promote neuropathways that reinforce intimacy; that is, it is analogous to *glue,* which strengthens the marriage relationship. Conversely, persistent sexual activity outside the marriage form pathways that distort a man's concept of a woman. For example, viewing naked women daily creates a neuropathway by which a man's normal attraction to sexual stimuli is distorted. His aberrant pathways, with time, may become permanent. All women become objects, including those fully dressed. Therefore, the effort to reverse sexual addiction becomes a significant challenge. The brain becomes distorted, and the demand for orgasm becomes accentuated. The addict navigates a sexual ship caught in a whirlpool—with no rescue in sight.

Dopamine activity begins in the limbic system, the most primitive part of the brain. Aberrant sexual behavior increases dopamine in the nucleus accumbens of the brain.

The nucleus accumbens houses nerve cells, positioned right below the cerebral cortex, called the *brain's pleasure center*. An addict describes a spike in dopamine as *motivation* or *pleasure* (Struthers 2009, p. 101). More accurately, dopamine signals feedback for predicted rewards. It increases sexual sensitivity and makes the addict long for a sexual partner. If a man perceives an attractive woman, his dopamine level will increase as his brain predicts a reward. When men and woman are sexually aroused by close contact, dopamine levels rise. At orgasm, the brain is flooded with dopamine, and it acts as a powerful mind-bending drug.

- **Norepinephrine.**

    Norepinephrine is both a hormone and a neurotransmitter. It increases sexual arousal and sexual memory. The effects are excitement and autonomic arousal that occur throughout the body in preparation for sexual activity (Struthers, 2009, pp. 101-102).

    It influences the reward system; it has sex enticing for both the man and woman.

    Norepinephrine is also responsible for stored emotional stimuli. For example, it sears into the brain images of the environment and sexual activity associated with a child's first exposure to sex. Often a child will remember his or her first encounter with sexual stimuli for a lifetime. It plays a role in impregnating stimulating pornographic images or behavior into a sex addict's memory. It also explains why partners in love can remember in detail each other's physical characteristic as well as past sexual encounters (Struthers, 2009, p. 103).

- **Serotonin**

 A neurotransmitter that contributes to feelings of well-being and satisfaction. It is released after climax, and it engenders a deep feeling of calmness and a release from stress (Kastleman, 2007). Serotonin also reduces appetite, improves mood, and suppresses pain perception. High levels of serotonin elevate mood but decrease sexual response in a man.

- **Endogenous opiates.**

These opiates, produced in the body, include endorphins, enkephalins, dynorphins, and endomorphins. The rush, feeling of euphoria, or release experienced during sexual orgasm relates to the infusion of endogenous opiates; that is, when semen is released, it occurs along with opiate activation. Endorphins work as *natural pain relievers*. Repeated activation of endogenous opiates results in tolerance in the form of diminished euphoria. When viewing pornography, they are linked to masturbation and the craving for more stimulation (Struthers, 2009, pp. 104-105).

- **Oxytocin.**

This hormone acts primarily as a neuromodulator in the brain. Oxytocin is released during orgasmic climax and acts as a natural tranquilizer, lowers blood pressure, reduces susceptibility to pain, promotes feelings of attachment, and induces sleep (Kastleman, 2007, p. 42). If testosterone fosters sexual desire, oxytocin binds a man to a woman. As such, Oxytocin is called the *joyful brain chemical* (Kastleman, 2007, pp. 41-42). As levels rise, couples hold hands, hug, and watch a romantic movie. While released slowly during sexual activity, larger quantities are released after orgasm—and result in sexual satisfaction and higher levels of trust (Struthers, 2009, p. 105).

> When humans experience skin-to-skin contact, touch releases oxytocin into the brain. Oxytocin is associated with feelings of well-being, pleasure, and attachment (Ferree, 2010, p. 51).

If an addict repeatedly views pornography, he will bond to an image and not to a person (Struthers, 2009, p. 105). As such, a habitual viewer of pornography finds greater sexual satisfaction in visual images than in marital relations.

- **Delta-FosB.**

Delta-FosB, in conjunction with Dopamine, is generated when a man or woman use an addictive stimulus such as cocaine or pornography. All addictive stimuli cause an increase in Delta-FosB. In non-technical terms, Delta-FosB sponsors a change, a rewiring of the brain, which causes a man and a woman to seek the pleasurable feelings that accompany drug or pornography use.

Delta-FosB increases' craving that traps the addict into escalating use. Researchers characterize the search as a quest for *unending novelty* (Wilson, 2009). Also, Delta-**FosB makes the addict prone to relapse**. These consequences explain why it is so difficult for the addict to end addictive behavior. The altered brain fights to continue its addictive state (Enth, 2001, p. 2).

Over time, the addict must view more stimulating pornography to get the same effect. This adaptation, perversely, dampens the pleasurable effects of sexual behavior. On the other hand, Delta-FosB increases sexual urges and corrals the addict into a destructive spiral of increasing use. The human brain facilitates the formation of an addictive state by the constant supply of powerful brain chemicals. A man and a woman can generate euphoric feelings solely by activating their own brain chemicals—without any outward sexual activity. Delta-FosB has extended consequences for the addict. It is endurable, that is, the feeling of sexual cravings remains active for weeks to months and some even much longer. The continuing feeling of sexual desire makes the addict subject to prolonged withdrawal (Nestler, Barrot, & Self, 2001, p. 1). Enth (2001) addressed withdrawal. The brain promotes the continuation of addictive behavior because of the discomfort the addict feels when he stops acting out (p. 2).

Association of systems

Sexual activity does not occur in a vacuum. It takes place at a location and at a selective time. These related systems remind the brain that the pleasure of sex is associated with the place, time, a person, smell, taste, etc. For example, an associated system for an alcoholic may be his neighborhood bar and his drinking friends. The alcoholic may tell himself that he is just going for an evening walk. However, if he walks anywhere near his favorite bar or encounters any of his drinking friends, his brain triggers an associative response, and his next drink is very near. Once the associative systems kick in, the alcoholic's power to resist is vastly reduced.

Likewise, the sex addict has associated systems that lure him back to sexual activity. For example, the man who is addicted to Internet pornography will convince himself he is only going online to check e-mail. However, his brain knows that the act of turning on the computer is the first step toward sexual pleasure. Once an e-mail is checked, the addict may tell himself he needs to check some other sites for whatever reason. The process continues until the addict finds a link that takes him down the road to pornography and acting out. Carnes (1994) calls this ritualization.

A sexually addicted man has difficulty changing his lifestyle so that associative systems are no longer part of his life. Such a lifestyle change can be difficult and may have high-priced consequences. If a man goes to the TV each evening in search of provocative images or scenes as a prelude to masturbation, giving away the TV may seem an unacceptable price. Placing filter software on a computer may affect legitimate as well as pornographic sites. The inability to link to legitimate sites is often used as an excuse not to block pornographic sites. Sobriety has a price.

Sexual fantasies

A sexually addicted man lives for exciting sexual fantasies. A man will see an attractive woman, store the images in his brain, and then construct a fantasy with that person. Sexual fantasies are part of the brain's indoctrination since they serve as a launching platform for acting out. Looking for new and exciting sexual fantasies becomes a way of life and occupies, much of the sex addict's time. Some sex addicts become so attached to the process they cannot go to sleep without their favorite fantasy. While sexual fantasies are most often used to arouse, they are also used to calm stress. Sexual fantasies produce a sense of euphoria. They medicate life's pain. Sexual fantasies are a large part of the addiction and are very difficult to let go once they have become habitual.

An abused person can also use sexual fantasies as a defense mechanism. Often when a child is traumatized by sexual abuse, the child's mind dissociates from reality. When the mind dissociates, it compartmentalizes what is happening in the present time and focuses on a mental sequence of another time and place or a fantasy or daydream absent of the pain of the present moment. The child uses dissociation to survive the trauma of abuse. Later in life, the dissociation skill may be used in the form of a pleasurable sexual fantasy.

Age appropriate time to expose children to human sexuality

You may wonder at what age is the appropriate time to expose children to human sexuality.

- Every age is appropriate to expose a child to healthy sexuality. No age is appropriate to expose a child to sexual arousal. Exposure to age-appropriate education and guidance should begin when a parent first sees a child exploring his or her genitals. Distracting a child who is touching his or her genitals is more appropriate than slapping the child's hands.
- Parental reaction to sexuality is critical to understanding the difference between abusive and healthy sexuality.

- When a child is found playing doctor with a similarly aged child, it is best to explain that God made us wonderfully, but it is better to keep our clothes on when playing with other children.
- It is an opportunity to share guidance about healthy sexuality when parents find a pornographic magazine hidden under a boy's mattress.

Redirect sexual behavior

When a child asks a question about sex, parents should answer the child's question in a way that creates a safe and healthy atmosphere. A thoughtful answer encourages the child to ask more questions as needed. Parents need to provide age-appropriate answers (Many books are available to help parents prepare to talk to their children about one of God's greatest gifts to humanity—sexuality).

Exposing a child to age-appropriate sexual instruction will help to preclude addiction. A child, who feels his parents are open to talking about sex, will feel free to confide in a parent if something untoward happens. When a parent can explain to the child that the behavior he or she experienced caused normal feelings as God intended, and the event was not his or her fault, the event will have far less impact. If the event is normalized, it is not likely to be a catalytic event.

On the other hand, parents (where one of the partners is addicted) tend to avoid discussions of sexuality because of the shame and guilt present in the family structure. This environment causes a child untoward curiosity and experimentation. Any sexually sterile environment creates a vacuum, which is likely to be filled. Extremes—an excessively sexualized environment or a sterile sexual environment—are fertile ground for sex addiction.

Internet pornography is affecting the minds of children at an alarming rate: so much so that some experts expect an epidemic of illicit sexual behavior. As a deterrent, the family computer must include blocking software to preclude access to pornography. Exposure to Internet pornography is rarely healthy. Just like a parent who would not allow a child to be exposed to a staph infection, a parent cannot allow the child to be exposed to pornography—even if the blocking software precludes adult access.

By reading this and other recommended books, you have become more aware of the destructive nature of age-inappropriate sexual material and activity. A change in your understanding will help you parent your children and preclude your child from falling victim to addiction.

**The chains of habit are
generally too small

to be felt until they

are too strong to

be broken.
Samuel Johnson**

Chapter Seven

OtherCharacteristics
of Sexual Addiction

This chapter explores how depressed mood, isolation, anger, and anxiety play a role in the life of an addicted man. As you process this chapter, ask yourself if the descriptions apply to your partner. Some will, and some may not.

Living in a low-grade depressed mood is a universal characteristic of those who are sexually addicted. It dominates their existence. Many addicts focus on what is going wrong in life rather than what is going right, a condition which fosters acting out.

The mental health community calls a chronic low-grade depressed mood a **Persistent Depressive Disorder**, or a **Dysthymic Disorder** (APA, 2013). While not much in life is upbeat, the addict can still function. To engage in frequent sexual behavior, guilt feelings convince him or her of being defective. Isolation is a consequence of living in a chronically depressed mood. Depressed mood and isolation tend to coexist. (Therapy for a person who masturbates to relieve chronic anxiety is different.)

- **Depressed mood**

Everyone experiences disappointment, failure, and the feeling of depressed mood. A student is disappointed for failing to study sufficiently to get a good grade on an exam. A codependent addict may feel a sense of abandonment when his wife chooses to spend her vacation with a friend. It is a normal function of life to have a bad day. For most, with time, the depressed mood passes. Healthy people experience normal bad days but do not use sexual behavior to raise their mood. On the other hand, addicts use sexual behavior to change their depressed mood.

Depressed mood is both a consequence of as well as a contributor to sexual addiction. Successfully treating depressed mood is part of ending aberrant sexual behavior. Symptoms of depressed mood span a continuum from mild to severe.

Some talk about their symptoms of depression but do not state their condition in terms of feelings. Absence of feelings creates numbness that masks the ability to experience joy and the positive aspects of life. Addicts are rarely in touch with their feelings.

Addicts can affect feelings in the way they think. Some thoughts generate very good feelings, such as anticipated marital sex or bad feelings such as rejection by a loved one. A man and woman have power over their feelings. Thus, they can change how they feel and think about life's experiences. Negative thoughts, often called **stinking thinking**, are automatic thoughts and cognitive distortions. Excuses, rationalizations, justifications are also cognitive distortions. Some stinking thinking is attached to youthful experiences, while other stinking thinking is the product of justifying aberrant behavior. When partners reject negative thinking, the outcome is more likely a positive control over their life. For example, if a couple engages in positive communications, the result is an important component of a loving relationship. On the other hand, poor communication drives a wedge between the couple. For instance, pessimistic automatic thoughts, particularly if they are unarticulated, are usually destructive because they lead to making unfounded assumptions. On the other hand, a recovery goal is to change negative automatic thoughts into positive cognitions, and thus, they become a source of constructive communication and energy. Ultimately, a choice is needed.

A classic use of stinking thinking by an addict is the belief one is entitled to immediate gratification at the onset of a sexual urge. Stinking thinking is illogical and a denial of responsibility. If the addict forgoes entitlement to immediate gratification, a choice to accept responsibility is a blessing. Lies dissolve and recovery is possible.

- **Chronically depressed mood**
Step back and view contrasting personas. Below is a series of alternatives. As you read the choices, decide if you are more like A or more like B.

  If you found answers in the B column describes you best, chronically depressed mood is part of your life.

✓	You are "A"	✓	You are "B"
	Always smiling		Rarely smiles
	Spend time with family.		Spends time with TV.
	Always has a joke to tell.		Rarely tells a joke.
	Rarely sulks.		Spends much time sulking
	Has many close friends		Has no or few friends
	Looks for new family things to do.		Works at house by self.
	Enjoys non-sex intimacy		No idea of non-sex intimacy
	Enjoys a lively conversation at the dinner table.		Rarely enjoys self is self-absorbed
	Is seen as a joyful person		Rarely experiences joy.

- Shame is likely a characteristic of your family of origin.

- Chronically depressed mood contributes to acting-out behavior.

- If as a child, your partner formed a habit of self-arousal, he accepted shame into the family self prevails over anything positive in his life.

- As a child, your partner did not receive the emotional nourishment he needed to develop into a healthy persona.

- If as a child, your partner formed a habit of self-arousal, he accepted shame into the family self prevails over anything positive in his life.

What is the greatest problem? Perhaps despair is the ultimate pitfall. When he continues sexual behavior, denying hope is his answer. After a slip, he justifies acting out again by all sorts of stinking thinking. To act out again is a form of despair and a defeatist attitude.

The death of a family member or a friend is usually a severe event and causes a depressed mood. With time, the depressed mood may subside. The most serious state of depression is full-scale that adversely affects the addict's ability to function. In its worst iteration, the addict requires hospitalization.

- **Dysthymic Disorder**

All sexually addicts suffer from low-grade depression. According to diagnostic criteria, Dysthymic Disorder, low-grade depression, lasts for at least two years, during which time the person experiences a continuous feeling of malaise (APA, 2013). For the addict, low-grade depression can last a lifetime.

Low-grade differs from full depression only to the degree of the impact on one's daily functioning. For example, a fully depressed person may be unable to sleep properly, eat, or concentrate. Conversely, an addict who suffers low-grade depression functions each day but thinks he or she is missing the joys of life and generally finds living a burden. Such a person wakes up and says, "Oh, God, not another day," instead of as would a healthy person say, "Good God, thanks for another day."

Living in low-grade depressed mood keeps an addict bound to sexual addiction. He or she awakens each morning to another day of few, if any, close friends, feeling lonely much of the time, procrastinates because of fear of failure, and looks for more from life but does not seem ever to find it. The state of malaise spans many adult years. It becomes painful, and the prospect of escape through sex is inviting. Sex becomes a way of self-medicating low-grade depressed mood.

Persistent feelings of shame and guilt accompany Dysthymic Disorder (APA, 2013). Chronically depressed addicts raise their mood by sexual stimulation, often by viewing pornography and engaging in masturbation.

Do you believe low-grade depressed mood is a by-product of shame experienced during long periods of acting out? Some of the symptoms are a loss of interest in daily activities, self-centeredness, isolation, cranky, and lack of energy, low self-esteem, self-criticism, or feeling of being unworthy. The addict tends to mitigate these symptoms. It can be a never-ending cycle.

While the *Diagnostic Statistical Manual (DSM)* criteria specify two year period; for addicts, the time is many years (APA, 2013). As such, addicts lack clarity as to the impact of the symptoms experienced since they have no comparison between a normal mood and a low-grade depressed mood. However, when asked if their partners exhibit the symptoms of low-grade depression, a woman's answer is usually an emphatic yes.

In this chapter, new concepts pertinent to the process of recovery includes the *Addict's Lifeline, Addict's Life Scale, "40" activities,* and *Living at "40".*

Addict's lifeline

Jean Piaget's stage theory asserts all humans undergo a common development through stages with defined beginning and ends. Responsible adults assist children in advancing through these stages (Santrock, 1995).

- **A *lifeline* begins at birth with attachment**

The *Addict's Lifeline* begins at birth, and the first stage is an attachment. It is essential newborns bond with a parent, most often the child's mother. The parent fosters attachment by actions the infant perceives as caring and security such as a mother singing to her baby; making eye contact and cooing with a sweet gentle, voice; playing with her baby's hands and feet; stroking the cheek, head, and cuddling; and bathing and frequent diaper changing.

The first *Lifeline stage* of development is the child's attachment. It is related to the ability of the parent to form a loving bond with the child. **Parental attachment** is an assurance that the child's physical, psychological, mental reasoning, and training and are in the good hands of care keepers. The effective attachment provides a base from which a child reaches out to develop reasoning, language, and training in life skills.

If a child does not experience attachment, the bond between child and mother is deficient; he or she as an adult will crave love and a caring relationship. Lack of attachment fosters needy adults who often marry sex addicts. A child may engage in sexual behavior as a substitute for attachment. Interestingly, the deficiency is also present in marital and other adult relationships.

• **Children three to six**

Children aged three to six are self-centered, as God intended. It is the time when children discover their own identity. As such, the focus is on mastering their environment and relationships. It is a time when temper tantrums tempt a parent to give into the child's wants.

• **Children six to thirteen**

During the next stage, parental deficiencies may contribute to a child's sexual behavior, age six through thirteen. Parental selfishness leads to abandonment. Abandonment fosters child sexual behavior when parents or other caregivers forsake a child by engaging in physical or sexual abuse; failing to care for the child's physical or mental health; or welfare or fails to provide emotional nourishment the child needs to be a whole and a functioning person.

Bradshaw calls such an existence as *barely surviving* in a dysfunctional family. During his stage, many children introduced to sexual behavior will progress into adult sexual addiction.

• **Teen to early adult**

During the next stage, teen to early adult, sexual behavior may become habitual. The young adult often branches out into other sexual activities.

During an addict's early adulthood, the addict's habitual behavior hardens his/her conscience. The addict acts-out compulsively, and behaviors grow in intensity. For some, acting out is not so much for pleasure, but to raise mood, quiet anxiety, subdue feelings of anger or loneliness, and boost low self-esteem.

- **All developmental phases**

A factor spans all the above developmental phases. A child often does not confide in parents as to his/her sexual exposure; the child lives in a secret state of isolation and dysfunction. Besides, the child has no concept of the consequences of aberrant sexual behavior. Unless an intervention provides insight, the child face's life as a sex addict. Sexual and emotional abuse influence how children maturate. Children left to fend for themselves often grow into adulthood emotionally stunted. They look like selfish adults who are overly attuned to getting their needs met. They have an overpowering need to repeat the soothing feelings from sexual behavior.

- **Adult**

Note: A presentation of *Living at "40"* follows the *Addict's Life Scale*. The origin of the concept, "40," is explained as part of the *Addict's Life Scale*. The *Living at "40"* concept and exercise were clinically tested and proved effective (Becker, 2012c, pp. 4-130).

Addict's Life Scale

Addicts are called to reject their addiction and strive to improve their quality of life. When addicts live at a normal *mood level, the "40" benchmark on the Addict's Life Scale*, their desire to act out decreases. Living at "20" increases the addict's desire to act out.

Later in the chapter an exercise, *Living at "40,"* provides an alternative to living in the low-grade depressed mood by practicing daily non-sexual intimacy. A table is provided for the partners to record their non-sexual intimacy activities. These activities, when practiced by the couple, help them live at a normal person's mood level, that is, at the "40" benchmark level on the *Addict's Life Scale.*

The *Addict's Life Scale* is used to visualize why an addict would choose to introduce "40 activities" into the marital relationship. Living at "40" improves the bond between partners and reduces the susceptibility to act out. The objective is to adopt healthy activities as a means of reducing negativity and thus acting out.

- **Fifty-point benchmark**

The *Addict's Life Scale* has a range of "0" to "50" in ten-point increments. Each benchmark on the scale correlates with a relative mood level. At the top of the scale is the "50" point benchmark. This level signifies the mood associated with the euphoria one feels during the buildup and orgasm.

- **Forty-point benchmark**

One step down is the forty-point benchmark. It is the mood level of a normal functioning person. The relationship between "50" and "40" point levels is, a person who achieves life at "40" will not act out to achieve the "50" benchmark. The jump of only 10 points is not worth the consequences. Life at "40," is very satisfactory. Ultimately the addict, who lives at the "20" point level is encouraged to incorporate new behaviors to function at the "40" level, and thus eliminate the need to raise his/her mood by acting out.

- **Thirty-point benchmark**

The next step down is the "30" point benchmark. A person visits the thirty-point benchmark but does not live there. It is called "bad hair day."

- **Twenty-point benchmark**

The addict lives at the "20" point benchmark. The addict functions at a low-grade depressed mood or *Persistent Depressive Disorder, Dysthymia* (APA, 2013). The addict looks for more from life but does not seem to discover it.

The addict plans to jump of 30 points; a jump from "20" to "50." The addict jumps 30 points to gain temporary relief from stress, chronic anxiety, depressed mood, anger, etc. He/she considers the euphoric experience is worth the relief. The addict rationalizes, acting out to feel better even for a short time, is just part of the addiction.

- **Ten-point benchmark**

The "10" point benchmark represents a person in a full-scale depressed mood. This person finds it difficult to eat, sleep, and go about daily life. An addict rarely experiences full-scale depressed mood. Addicts are survivors.

- **Zero-point-benchmark**

  The "0" point benchmark represents a person who will or has spent time in an institution. At the "0" point benchmark, a person is no longer in control of life.

The important points are:

Those who live at the "40" point level live a normal non-addictive life. A ten-point jump as hardly worth the negative consequences. The "40" point level person engages in relationship building and, in turn, fosters a loving and supportive marriage. The "40" point level person does not need to act out to enjoy life.

The contrast between the "20" point level, where the addict lives, and the "50" point level, is a jump of 30-points. After the addict has acted out, his mental condition returns to the depressed mood level (the "20" point level). For the man who acts outs, the jump to "50" is a relief from life's pain. The pain is so unacceptable; the addict is willing to go for a short-term fix.

The conclusion of the *Addict's Life Scale* is the 20-point addict needs to join others who live at "40." This means the addict must stop acting out and begin to engage in "40" activities to improve one's life and marriage.

Now, if the addict engages in the same relationship-building behaviors as does a normal "40" point level person, the supposition is the addict does not need to act out to enjoy life. It does not mean more frequent sex.

Improving relations with one's partner is key to a satisfying life. Addicts who learn to practice non-sexual intimacy at home and loving intimacy in the marriage bed have found the Holy Grail. Non-sexual intimacy is the kindnesses a normal adult chooses to do for his/her partner with no expectation of a return on investment. For example, non-sexual intimacy activities include bringing home a rose, purposely setting time aside to talk, taking a walk, reading a book together, going to the gym together, and going out to dinner.

Non-sexual intimacy means your partner treats you **as number one, that is he makes you, first.** For a long time, the addict put self first to meet his/her sexual needs. That must change! Sex is the desert, not the meal's nutrition. Marital sex is best as part of a relationship-based, non-sexual intimacy.

New relationship model

You and your partner need to improve how the two of you relate to one another. For the addict, and from an early age, sexual intimacy meant engaging in aberrant behavior. An addict has no idea what a blessing non-sexual intimacy can mean in a changed life.

The following are the characteristics of "40 activities" plan.

- The plan spans a week, is committed to writing, and is posted to the family refrigerator as a visual reminder of both partner's commitment. (If it is just verbal the addict may procrastinate and fail to fulfill his/her commitment. Most addicts need external motivation to overcome mood-induced ambivalence.)

- Both partners work together to prepare their plan-usually over the weekend.

- The plan includes "no or low-cost" non-sexual activities for each day. If there is a notable cost to one or more of the activities, the exercise will fail.

- It is not the role of non-addicted partner to coerce the addict to fulfill his/her commitment. However, the non-addicted partner has a stake in changing how they relate to each other.

- While engaged in healthy activities, a couple's mood level rises. They perceive what normal feels like; a new experience for a sex addict.

If the "40 activities" plan frustrates the partners, they are encouraged to seek counseling. Their marital issues are likely deeper than frustration over the activities plan. Ideally, for each day of the week, the partners plan healthy joint activities. The activities vary according to the needs of the couple. Although the plan is composed primarily of non-sexual activities, it may, if necessary, include an instance of sexual intimacy. Marital relations affirm sexual intimacy as still part of the marital bond— **when and if both partners so desire**.

An activity plan restores a positive way of forming an intimate friendship lost when sex became a high priority during courting. An addict's entitlement thinking further distanced the couple. In recovery, couples go back to square one and build the friendship they should have built during courting. Married couples who, engaged in continuing friendship building do not deal with sexual addiction—they live at "40."

Living at "40."

Below is a representation of relationship-building activities for the weekly plan. However, doing so requires an agreement to work together. It requires a new paradigm in which the couple, while not forgetting past transgressions, are free to put aside their pain while they work together. To summarize so far: to raise mood and reduce acting out, the addict's goal is to live like a normal healthy person. This is called living at "40."

Daily activities vary according to the needs of the couple on a **"40" activities chart.**

"40" activities planning — for example

Sunday	Monday	Tuesday	Wednesday	Thursday	Friday	Saturday
Worship Family Activity Prepare written plan for the coming week	Take a Walk together and hold hands	Go to the gym and work out together	Discuss a book that both are reading **If both agree** - Marital Relation	Watch a movie together near each other No marital relations	Pizza and beer night Dinner at a low-cost food place	Family activity with or w/o children

Living at the forty-point level is taking different steps and is unique to each couple, but some additional common steps include:

- Be active in a club or church.
- Engage in healthy recreation.

- Carve out time each week to enjoy life such as biking, walking, playing with one's children, taking one's partner out to dinner, etc.

- Engage your partner or friend in good conversation. Start with fifteen minutes a day and continue to add time. Aim for a good hour of conversation each day.

- Call one or more friends every day. Cultivate a strong friendship.

- Focus on what is going right in your life and not what is going wrong.

- Serve others. As part of coming out of isolation, a recovering addict can choose to serve others. For example, consider serving periodically at a soup kitchen, volunteer at hospital, coach sports, or join a prison ministry.

  Below is a "40 activities" worksheet for you and your partner to copy and use. Your daily activities vary according to your needs. Add your examples of non-sexual intimacy to the chart below.

Your "40 activities" spreadsheet

Mon day	Tuesday	Wednes day	Thursday	Friday	Saturday	Sunday

Describe ten "40 activities" you would include on a weekly plan.

Describe ten "40 activities" your partner would include on a weekly plan.

What are the benefits you perceive from the "40 activities" exercise?

Do you perceive difficulty maintaining your commitment week after week?

What can you do to raise your commitment to follow the "40 activities" exercise?

What are your thoughts about the concept of Living at "40"?

Would you and your partner commit to the discipline and desire to use the "40 activities" plan for six months?

**People can't live with change
if there's not a changeless core
inside them. The key to the ability
to change is a changeless sense
of who you are, what you are
about and what you value.**

Stephen Covey

Chapter Eight

Codependency

To begin this chapter, a few thoughts may help.

- Clinical experience has shown that addicts tend to marry into a codependent relationship. Codependency will affect the marriage and may affect recovery. Both partners may find it beneficial to examine their role in the marriage.

- The term codependency was first coined in the Alcoholic Anonymous community. Codependency is defined as the propensity of marriage partners to look for happiness or the lack of contentment based on the behavior of the partner. In simpler terms, each partner expects the other partner to cause his or her happiness. Melody Beattie (1992), a well-known author, defines codependency as:

A codependent person is one who has let another person's behavior affect him or her, and who is obsessed with controlling that person's behavior.

- We noted earlier that the sexually addicted man did not have a nourishing relationship with his father—and in some cases, with his mother. Bradshaw (1988) relates:

> Co-dependence is the most common family illness because it is what happens to anyone in any dysfunctional family. In every dysfunctional family, there is a primary stressor. This could be Dad's drinking or work addiction; Mom's hysterical control of everyone's feelings; Dad or Mom's physical or verbal violence; a family member's sickness or hypochondriasis; Dad or Mom's early death; their divorce; Dad or Mom's moral/religious righteousness; Dad or Mom's sexual abuse. Anyone, who becomes controlling in the family to the point of being experienced as a threat by the other members, initiates the dysfunction

This chapter is not intended to assess blame on one or both partners. It merely conveys the reality in many relationships involving an addicted person. If after you read this chapter and you believe you are in a codependent relationship, then you are fortunate to recognize your situation. With knowledge comes the choice to change what is not working in your relationship.

To explore how codependency affects marriages, we have two stories. The stories include many of the characteristics found in codependent relationships.

Story number one: Jim and Barbara.

(The story begins with) Jim and Barbara's codependency characteristics - evident before marriage.

Jim dated while he was in high school for social conformity. Since he had not witnessed respectful interactions between his parents, his relationship skills were also lacking. He did not know what it meant to know and appreciate a person of the opposite sex. Outside of school dances and similar functions, his before marriage social life focused primarily on "making out." While "making out" never progressed beyond heavy petting, it was not for the lack of desire on his part.

Barbara also dated in high school. The man she dated was several years older and in the military. For her, the relationship was safe because of the distance and infrequency of face-to-face contact. Having experienced a dysfunctional family environment, she too lacked understanding of a healthy relationship. She had a sense of loneliness because she often disagreed with her parents.

Jim and Barbara's parents were alike in many ways. Neither set of parents showed much affection. Jim's father was an alcoholic. Barbara and Jim felt their parents loved them, but external signs of affection were rare. When Jim left for college, the message he believed his parents sent was, anything short of a high level of performance was unacceptable. Barbara's motivation is based on an internal perception that her parents would not love her if she failed in her academic pursuits.

Barbara and Jim met at college. The college sponsored mixers for incoming freshman and upperclassmen were open for all to attend. Jim felt an immediate attraction to Barbara. To him, she had all the physical attributes that met his criteria for an attractive girl. He felt she was a bit naïve but thought it was cute. On the other hand, while she thought Jim was reasonably attractive, she was not particularly interested in dating him. She had not planned to get involved with a college man because her studies were more important to her.

Jim invited Barbara to campus social affairs and fraternity parties. The first several times, she turned him down. She finally agreed to go to a fraternity mixer. By this time, Jim was very attracted to Barbara. He dreamed of having a steady relationship with her. Several months after their initial encounter, their relationship turned sexual. Once sexual activity entered into their relationship, neither seemed to put a priority on developing a strong non-sexual friendship. The glue that held the relationship together was a physical and emotional dependency on each other.

Jim and Barbara dated for several years before they married. During this time, Jim's sexual needs continued to grow while Barbara tried to satisfy her need for love by giving into Jim's need.

Codependency characteristics flourish in marriage

Jim and Barbara married and began a family. A year or so into the marriage, it became very apparent to Barbara that Jim was manipulative. His needs always seemed to come first. Joint decisions were often the product of Jim's persuasion. While he was a good economic provider, as a loving companion, he was far from ideal. Barbara felt very alone in the marriage and focused all her attention on raising their children. She tried numerous times to talk to him about her needs and her perception of a loving marriage. He repeatedly made promises to do better but did not do so. His perception was, as long as he provided a good economic subsistence for the family, he fulfilled his end of the bargain. Because he felt Jim and Barbara's parents were alike in many ways. Neither set of parents showed much affection. Jim's father was an alcoholic. Barbara and Jim felt their parents loved them, but external signs of affection were rare. When Jim left for college, the message he believed his parents sent was, anything short of a high level of performance was unacceptable. Barbara's motivation is based on an internal perception that her parents would not love her if she failed in her academic pursuits.

Barbara and Jim met at college. The college sponsored mixers for incoming freshman and upperclassmen were open for all to attend. Jim felt an immediate attraction to Barbara. To him, she had all the physical attributes that met his criteria for an attractive girl. He felt she was a bit naïve but thought it was cute. On the other hand, while she thought Jim was reasonably attractive, she was not particularly interested in dating him. She had not planned to get involved with a college man because her studies were more important to her.

Jim invited Barbara to campus social affairs and fraternity parties. The first several times, she turned him down. She finally agreed to go to a fraternity mixer. By this time, Jim was very attracted to Barbara. He dreamed of having a steady relationship with her. Several months after their initial encounter, their relationship turned sexual. Once sexual activity entered into their relationship, neither seemed to put a priority on developing a strong non-sexual friendship. The glue that held the relationship together was a physical and emotional dependency on each other.

Jim and Barbara dated for several years before they married. During this time, Jim's sexual needs continued to grow while Barbara tried to satisfy her need for love by giving into Jim's very self-centered and *need.*

Codependency characteristics flourish in marriage

Jim and Barbara married and began a family. A year or so into the marriage, it became very apparent to Barbara that Jim was very self-centered and manipulative. His needs always seemed to come first. Joint decisions were often the product of Jim's persuasion. While he was a good economic provider, as a loving companion, he was far from ideal. Barbara felt very alone in the marriage and focused all her attention on raising their children. She tried numerous times to talk to him about her needs and her perception of a loving marriage. He repeatedly made promises to do that Barbara constantly suggested ways in which he needed to improve, he shied away from a give and take discussions because he feared he would see himself as a failure. Jim and Barbara grew apart in their marriage.

More than a decade into their marriage, Barbara learned that Jim had been unfaithful. Jim had marital affairs with several women at work and was addicted to pornography. In one long evening, he confessed all his transgressions and begged for Barbara's forgiveness. Jim insisted he would become a new man. Jim initially felt relieved that his greatest and most shameful secrets were exposed. The stress of leading a secret, dual life had become almost intolerable.

His promise to become a new man was short lived. He kept a secret stash of pornographic material for his periodic fix. In the deep recesses of his mind, he reasoned, as he had done in the past, manipulate Barbara into accepting his promise to change his ways—and move on. Not this time! Barbara now recognized his manipulative behavior and was not satisfied with his explanations, or his promises. Barbara was angry and decided she was not going to let Jim get away with what he had done to her and their family. She embarked on a plan to hold him accountable to his promise to change his behavior.

Jim wondered if the cure was worse than the disease. He contemplated leaving Barbara but was terrified with the thought of being alone and isolated from his children. He hoped that Barbara's fury would abate with time, but he was wrong.

Barbara also wondered whether she wanted to stay in the marriage. "Was it worth it," she asked herself. She contemplated leaving Jim but was confounded by the thought of being financially insecure and having to raise the children by herself. She convinced herself to stay until the children were in college. She made plans to get a job so she could grow financially independent. She saw Jim as a selfish "bastard" who was out to get his sexual needs met notwithstanding the total disregard for the marriage covenant. While she did not put it in terms of "punishment," she felt he had it coming when she monitored his every move. She had given up hope of ever trusting him again. Yet, deep down, she felt she needed him and the security that he provided. She saw Jim as a pathetic sex monger and herself as the victim of his total selfishness.

Jim and Barbara's marriage had hit rock bottom. Both were very angry people living under the same roof and incapable of seeing a way out of their dysfunctional relationship.

Jim and Barbara were living in a codependent destructive world. Both were living under false premises. Jim thought his future happiness lay in Barbara, agreeing to love him for whom he was without her trying to change him. Barbara saw her future happiness as a product of a reinvented Jim, and she was going to take charge of his reinvention. Barbara was not going to be successful in changing Jim. Only Jim could change Jim. Sex could no longer be his greatest need. Jim's good friend suggested he consider getting help. On his own volition, Jim entered sex addiction counseling and participated in an accompanying Twelve-Step program. Jim's recovery would take time, and he would have to grieve the damage he had done to himself and all those around him.

Marital therapy would be needed to reestablish trust, friendship, and a spiritual connection in the marriage. The healing journey will take years. Since Jim and Barbara contemplated divorce, if they do not invest fully in the recovery program, they are doomed to repeat the same failures in any subsequent marriage. Ultimately, with therapy and commitment, they can find the relationship both want and need in their present marriage.

Codependency characteristics in Jim and Barbara's marriage.

The following are characteristics of codependency found in Jim and Barbara's story. You may or may not find yourselves in their story, but the principles set below mirror the experiences of many couples where the male is addicted.

Characteristic # 1: The origin of codependency is in a child's dysfunctional family.

Parents of codependent children are often codependent themselves, as were Jim and Barbara's parents. The traits are handed down, that is, taught to each succeeding generation. The parents of the codependent children are ill-equipped to provide emotional nourishment to their children. Instead, dysfunctional families abound in addiction, narcissism, and the inability to show love to their children. Internally focused parents are ill-equipped to build healthy relationships with their children. They cannot give what they do not have.

Jim's father was an alcoholic. As such, he was not present to the developmental needs of his son. Jim learned from his father how to be self-centered. He learned that earning his father's love was based on his performance. His father looked to Jim to succeed where he perceived he failed in life. Jim's mother was a codependent enabler of her husband's alcoholism; that is, she continued to purchase alcohol for her husband. Jim could not get his emotional needs met from his family of origin. While he was unable to codify it as a child, as an adult, he recognized that he was emotionally detached and abandoned by his parents. His emotional deficiency led him to focus on satisfying his needs without regard to the needs of those around him.

From his parents, Jim also learned to manipulate others into meeting his needs. He used dominance to trump normal healthy interactions in his relationships. He was unable to be a friend and have empathy for others. Jim was also abused as a child at the hands of an older sibling. As he grew older, he turned auto-arousal to foster feelings of well-being. He substituted sexual satisfaction for friendship and respect in his relationships.

Barbara's father was emotionally distant from his family. His work and weekend golf took precedence over his family. If he had a choice, he chose to be absent from his wife and children. When Barbara was a teenager, her mother often talked about wanting to leave her husband but never did. Barbara now recognizes that her parents were in a codependent relationship. Barbara did not experience a sense of well-being from her parents. She felt she had to earn parental love. Among her siblings, she was the caretaker and the responsible child.

Both Jim and Barbara were predestined to enter into a codependent relationship.

Characteristic # 2: Children of codependent dysfunctional families have ill-formed or incomplete personalities.

Adult behavior, either intentionally or not, builds on the   dysfunctional personality traits learned in the family of origin.

Jim often felt deficient in his social skills and questioned his self-worth. Because of low self-esteem, he often wondered if anyone really could love him. Nevertheless, his distorted thinking led him to equate sex with a feeling of being loved. Through his previous experience with erotic arousal, he sought mood escalation through masturbation. It never occurred to Jim that there was much more to a relationship than sex. After all, he reasoned, if a girl would participate in sexual activity with him, surely, they loved each other.

Barbara's hole in the soul was her need to be loved. In response to the attention she received from Jim, she allowed herself to be manipulated into an early sexual relationship. From time to time, she felt sex occupied far too much of their relationship. Several times, she attempted to establish what she considered more healthy boundaries. She was no match for Jim's manipulative skills.

Jim's attraction to Barbara focused on her attractive body parts. He lacked the insight needed to focus on her personality and personhood. He felt that the essence of a steady relationship was to have Barbara depend on him. While Barbara frequently felt uneasy, she also lacked the skills to evaluate their relationship objectively. She bought into depending on him for an active college social life. After all, he was a fraternity brother, and she wore his pin.

Characteristic # 3: In marriage, codependency fosters pain and negativity.

Once married, Jim's eyes began to wander. He needed the thrill of pursuing a new conquest. He began to repeat the cycle he originated with Barbara while they were in college. Jim lacked marriage skills, and his pursuits outside of the marriage bed further distanced him from providing the emotional nourishment Barbara so dearly needed.

Barbara substituted her desire for marital happiness by focusing her attention on her children. Her friends saw her as an outstanding and dedicated mother. She tried to meet her children's every need. Barbara transferred her dependence on Jim to reliance on her children for her emotional well-being. She tried to fill the hole in her soul by forming a bond with her children. However, children are unable to return love, as would a healthy adult.

Jim continued to insist on sex with Barbara. She feared to say "no" because she was afraid of Jim's anger. Barbara felt disconnected from Jim. She gave him what he wanted, but she felt she was simply paying dues.

Characteristic # 4: Fear, shame, anger, and depressed mood are companions of codependency

Jim continued to live in two worlds—one foot outside his marriage and one foot inside. While he believed he was clever enough not to be caught, he realized that his life was out of control and getting worse. He was ashamed and lived in a low-grade depressed mood. He knew that his relationship with Barbara had gone from good to bad, but he had no idea how to change it. He did not intend to give up his best friend, sex. After all, for some reason, a man needs some pleasure in life.

When Barbara learned of Jim's closely held secrets, she felt conflicting emotions. On the one hand, she was relieved to learn that her suspicions of Jim's infidelity were real; she was not crazy. On the other hand, she was outraged and felt great anger. She was also dominated by fear. She was fearful she would be left very alone in life: what would become of her and the children? How could anyone understand the intense feeling of betrayal she felt? She was so depressed that getting out of bed each day, eating, and caring for the children seemed like monumental tasks.

Characteristic # 5: Codependency is part of the problem.

For Jim and Barbara, codependency was an integral part of their marriage. Jim depended on his ability to manipulate Barbara, so he could continue to get his needs met. Barbara depended on her anger to respond to Jim's betrayal of their marriage contract. Their illusions of happiness lie in the performance of the other party.

Neither would be successful.

Both would benefit from counseling. Jim needed to address his addictive behavior. Barbara would do well to seek counseling to address the trauma of her marital relationship. They both need help to resolve the present crisis and to help support the family.

Story number two: Joe and Alice's marriage.

Joe, a mid-level executive, had multiple affairs during his twenty years of marriage to Alice. It was usual for Joe to have more than one affair going at the same time. While his marriage to Alice provided him with two wonderful children, he continued his liaisons. He said, "I don't feel particularly close to Alice. She does her thing, and I do mine."

Joe password protected his computer and e-mail accounts. One evening he inadvertently left his e-mail account open. Alice stumbled onto Joe's e-mail exchanges with his ladies. **Pandemonium ensued**.

Alice demanded full disclosure. Joe complied but refused to give sufficient details to satisfy Alice. Joe felt he did not want to cause more pain than he had already caused. He also talked about the shame of his behavior and his fear that Alice would leave him if she knew the details. Alice wanted a full accounting of all his transgressions, and to keep her abreast of his sexual thinking and behavior daily. She was angry and terrified. She felt betrayed and was concerned about the future of their marriage and the raising of their children.

Neither Joe nor Alice wanted a divorce, but the bond between them was fractured. Joe said that for years, he wanted to let Alice in on his most guarded secrets of infidelity but feared she would try to fix him or leave him. In fact, his fears became a reality. Alice, in her despondency, did everything she could to hold Joe accountable to her perception of a good marriage. In her zeal to monitor Joe, she obtained his credit card and telephone records for as many years as she could. She questioned any call that was not readily recognizable. She constantly accused him of going back to being unfaithful. She insisted on obtaining the phone number for each of the women with whom he had been unfaithful. She called every one of them to make it clear that Joe was no longer available. She embarrassed him by talking about what a rotten person he was to anyone who would listen—at his work, church, and community.

Alice continued to demand more information and frequently asked questions about one or more of his affairs. Periodically Joe would provide the detail of an affair, which then resulted in Alice berating him for the content of the detail. After each disclosure, she yelled that she could not trust him because she did not know how much more he had not told her.

They discussed their behavior in a joint marital therapy session. Alice and Joe made promises to change, but they did not. Their marriage therapist speculated that Alice had a hole in her soul related to sexual abuse as a child. In other words, she had her own shame. Shame binds Joe to Alice unless they deal with the roots of their dysfunction from childhood; it is unlikely the marriage will survive.

The other side of the coin.

Perhaps you identify with the steps Alice took to reclaim her partner. After all, what was wrong with her taking positive action? Why shouldn't she demand accountability from him? Why shouldn't she demand that he confess his transgressions in real time, so she could know how sincere he was in his promise to change? After all, she is the victim of his profound selfishness—putting his needs ahead of everything dear and sacred to the marriage contract.

The answer?

Alice is justified in her anger. However, if Joe is not committed to change his behavior and to hold himself accountable, Alice's efforts are headed for frustration and divorce. Joe must see that putting his sexual needs ahead of all else has a dim future.

Sexual addiction is a shame-based disease. Alice's actions add to Joe's shame. While hardly an excuse to justify acting-out behavior, shame, and feelings of worthlessness, often contribute to the addict's low-grade depression. Joe self-medicates negative feelings and low-grade depression through masturbation. One of the tasks he needs to address during recovery is exposing his sense of shame to the light of day.

Group and Twelve-step programs seek to counter the negativity. An essential step is to learn to live at the forty-point benchmark level by taking positive steps to come out of isolation, allowing shame to recede, and to forgo living in low-grade depression. Perhaps one could argue that Joe deserves to feel guilt and shame but doing so will not help him on his recovery journey.

Visual picture of Joe and Alice's codependency relationship.

Picture two elevators side by side: Joe occupies one and Alice the other. When Alice's elevator is on the tenth floor, Joe's elevator is in the basement. When Joe's elevator is in the basement, he sees himself as the errant child. He looks up to Alice on the tenth floor and sees a scornful mother. Joe gives Alice the power to chastise, for he believes he deserves it but intensely resents her doing so. Alice takes power given to her and dutifully scolds and punishes. She is no longer the spouse but has taken the role of Jim's codependent dysfunctional mother.

They ride their elevators to the opposite levels. Alice's elevator is now in the basement, and Joe's is on the tenth floor. Alice sees herself as the victim of Joe's self-centeredness. She sees his behavior as willful, destructive to the marriage, and selfish. She sees him in a superior position—doing his own thing without regard to the consequences, particularly to the marriage. Joe supports her vision by continuing to put his sexual needs first.

Joe and Alice continue to ride their respective elevators, alternating between the basement and tenth floor. As they ride, their anger grows, and they blame each other for their predicament.

What needs to change?

In simplistic terms, both Joe and Alice would do well to ride their elevators to the fifth floor, get off, and face one another.

Ideally, Joe admits he is powerless to stop his behavior—it has become unmanageable. His fifth-floor position is to thank Alice and to commit to counseling. His therapist will likely recommend he attend one or multiple Twelve-step programs regularly.

Alice rejects the role of Joe's mother. Alice tells Joe, "It is not my job to change you. That is your challenge." If so inclined, she can tell him, "I will pray for you. If you would like a friendly ear while you are in therapy, I may agree to listen, but I am not willing to be your accountability partner or try to fix you."

Alice may choose to deal with the origins of her codependent behavior in individual or group therapy.

Jonathan and Grace's Story

This story shows how one person's codependency can cause family grief.

Their story sounds like a typical, well-adjusted family, except for the temper tantrums Martha throws whenever her father is home. She feels that since she has reached the ripe age of sixteen, she is entitled to have a car of her own. Her father does not argue with her when she asks. He says, no. His no is usually followed by Martha's accusations of how mean her parents are, how they make her so unhappy, topped off with great tears and slamming of her bedroom door.

Jonathan and Grace enjoy their four children, but they sometimes wonder if joy is the right sentiment. The ages of their children and a characteristic of each are:

- Martha is a headstrong sixteen-year-old. While she makes good grades and does not cause problems at school, home is a different story.

- Jake, twelve, spends many of his waking hours reading Star Wars, Harry Potter, and similar age-appropriate books. He does very well in school. He is the apple of his mother's eye.

- Andy, eight, seems to be the lost soul. He is always telling his parents that he cannot find anything to do around the house. No suggestion satisfies him. However, he does enjoy playing with Ruff, the family dog. They take adventure trips together in the local woods. He also loves to visit his grandmother, who lives a few blocks away. His grandmother spoils the daylights out of him.

- Sarah, six, is the princess of the family. She changes clothes at least five times a day and, also, gets great delight from playing with her friends in the big clothes box in the attic. She is the apple of her father's eye.

- Martha is still young and does not realize she is engaging in fruitless codependent behavior. She looks forward to throwing her temper tantrums and telling the world (her stuffed animals) how her parents make her so unhappy. Fortunately, most teenagers grow out of difficult years.

The definition of codependency is allowing someone outside yourself to make you unhappy. Martha has the scenario down pat. Dad says no, and she lets all in hearing distance know that her dad is very mean. She is so put upon and is soooo unhappy. Do you recognize codependency scenarios at your home?

Codependency addressed.

In a healthy marriage, partners see themselves neither in a superior position nor as to the victim but as equals. Each takes individual responsibility to grow in wisdom. The male's goal is to accept that he has a problem, which he commits to addressing. The woman's goal is to accept that she, too, has issues she could address. They support each other in a quest to become whole and shun the paralyzing effects of shame.

In a codependent relationship, each partner's identity lies outside of the self. Each depends on the other to provide wholeness. Neither is independent in the relationship. For example, if you would like to change your partner's behavior, you are saying, "For me, happiness lies in how my partner can change, not on how I function independently." In a codependent relationship, both parties want to be in charge, but neither party feels that they are, and yet, each party feels the other is in charge.

A practical way to change your codependent response is to ask your partner how s/he is dealing with such and such a situation. Thank

him/her for his/her thoughts and tell him/her you will pray for him/her. Tell him/her you have issues on which you want to work as well. Tell him/her you are open to hearing what s/he has learned or interested in what s/he wants to share. Do not let yourself engage in a codependent response. Advice giving is not part of answer.
If your partner attempts to give you advice, ask him/her to tell you how it would change him/her if you followed his/her advice. Thank him/her for sharing and tell him/her that you need to pray on what you heard. You are now free to either make the change or not. Just because someone asks for something does not mean it's forthcoming.

The difference in the above behavior is you have introduced loving independence.

Two more considerations:

- While it is far from ideal, clinical experience has shown that the majority of those who enter addiction therapy do so because their partner has set a boundary that includes getting help.

- The vast majority of men cannot follow the recovery road by themselves. For the most part, any reasoning, which purports to the opposite, is a rationalization and contains elements of manipulation.

What else can I read about codependency?

The following books are well worth reading.

Codependent No More: How to Stop Controlling Others and Start Caring for Yourself by Melody Beattie, Hazelden Publishing; 2nd edition (September 1, 1992).

From the book cover:

By its nature, alcoholism and other compulsive disorders create victims out of everyone close to the afflicted person. Whether the person you love is an alcoholic, a gambler, a foodaholic, a workaholic, a sexaholic, a criminal, a rebellious teenager, or a neurotic parent, this book is for the codependent. This overview of codependency by Melody Beattie, a recovering alcoholic and former chemical dependency counselor, details the dependency characteristics, where the behavior comes from, and how it affects those around us. Offering hope and guidance, *Codependent No More* discusses several options for controlling behavior and helps us understand that letting go will set us free.

Facing Codependence: What It Is, Where It comes from, How It Sabotages Our Lives by Pia Melody with Andrea Wells Miller and J Keith Miller. Harper & row; 1st edition (May 17, 1989).

From the book cover: In codependency, Pia Melody traces the origins of this illness back to childhood, describing a whole range of emotional, spiritual, intellectual, physical, and sexual abuses. Because of these earlier experiences, codependent adults lack the skills necessary to lead mature lives and have satisfying relationships.

John Bradshaw focuses on the dynamics of the family, how the rules and attitudes learned while growing up becoming encoded with each family member. As 96% of all families are, to some degree, emotionally impaired, the unhealthy rules we are now living by are handed down from one generation to another and ultimately to society at large. Our society is sick because our families are sick. Our families are sick because we are living by inherited roles that we never wrote. *Women, Sex, and Addiction: A Search for Love and Power* by Charlotte Sophia Kasl Harper Paperbacks; 1st, First edition (July 5, 1990)

From the book cover:

In our society, sex is the price a man and a woman pay for love and the illusion of security. A woman who seeks a sense of personal power and an escape from the pain may use sex and romance as a way to feel in control, just as alcoholics use alcohol; but sex never satisfies her longing for love and self-worth. In this book, Kasl shows women how they can learn to experience their sexuality as a source of love and positive power and sex as an expression that honors the soul as well as the body.

Find additional titles in Appendix C.

It is common for addicts to live in a fantasy world. For the most part, they believe in the illogical: I will never be caught, and if I am caught, I will minimize my sexual behavior. A cartoon by Zuzu Galifianakis (2011) gives us insight into male thinking. The cartoon shows a man and woman in which the male says, "I never meant to hurt you. My plan was always to get away with it." The logic expressed in the cartoon is so on target when it applies to pornography addiction, the subject of the next chapter.

**Self-respect is the root
of discipline; the sense
of dignity grows with the
ability to say no to oneself.**

Abraham J. Herschel

**Treat your mind like a bad neighborhood
— do not go there alone.**

Source Unknown

Chapter Nine

Pornography

Pornography is the millstone around the neck of an addicted man. Perhaps the number one reason a man enters therapy is to deal with pornography. Most have been caught viewing pornography online by their partner, significant other, or employer.

A man craves returning to the secrecy of sexual arousal that occurred during childhood. He mistakenly believes he can go online and enjoy his own secret world of sexual stimulation and never be caught. A man often repeats a pattern of staying up late—after his partner has gone to sleep—and searches the Internet for sexually stimulating images.

Bart describes the impact of viewing pornography on his marriage.

Bart believed viewing online pornography did not affect his marriage. Bart was an upward mobile young executive and often took work home. He had an agreement with his wife that he would not do office work while she and the children were awake. After Bart's wife retired for the evening, Bart went online. He would spend an hour or two attending to office work but then succumbed to the temptation to view pornographic material. He felt he deserved to reward himself, for he made lots of money, and his wife did not seem to need marital pleasure as much as he did. He looked forward to viewing pornography and subsequent masturbation.

His wife was a sound sleeper and never disturbed his late-night computer sessions. That was, until one night when she walked in on him and grasped, what she called "sick" images on his computer. Not only did she see the images on his computer but also Bart was in the process of masturbating when she walked in. Bart's wife, like any normal wife, was traumatized by her husband's behavior.

She told him that unless he got help, their relationship was likely over. Bart was devastated. He entered therapy but found the road to sexual sobriety more difficult than he expected. After a year in therapy, Bart continued three times a week attendance at a Twelve Step program to keep himself straight. He also found that an exercise program helped him maintain a better mental disposition. Having been discovered, Bart said, was initially the worst thing that could have happened to him. He now realizes it was the opportunity for life-changing choices and a far better relationship with his wife.

Roger searches for pornography from his work computer and believes his boss will overlook the work computer usage rules.

Roger was an IT person who believed he could defeat any filter or tracking tools used by his employer. His employer was a State government. However, system controls installed by his employer did not cause Roger to lose his "dream" position. One Friday afternoon, he was called into his supervisor's office and told to pack up his things. He was no longer an employee. His supervisor explained to him that a female coworker filed a sexual harassment complaint after she observed pornographic images on Roger's computer as she passed by his work cubicle. Roger was devastated. His wife was outraged. The family was in crisis. A major problem faced by the family was paying for the medical care of their disabled son. Roger was able to obtain freelance work that barely kept the family afloat. Roger and his family paid a high price for the lure of pornographic images.

TP's story is like Roger's story.

TP's employer made it clear; anyone caught viewing pornography at the work site would be fired. TP was a highly specialized engineer who thought, no matter what he did, he would never be fired. His company needed his expertise. TP's pattern of behavior was to view online pornography after his coworkers left for the day. He was caught and told by his boss that he had one more chance. He failed to take stock in the warning. He was subsequently fired for his activity on a company computer. TP entered therapy to try to convince his boss he was serious about changing his behavior. TP learned it was not his boss that he needed to satisfy but himself. He made good progress in therapy and works for another company.

The simplistic approach toward a definition means any material a man uses to foster sexual arousal is pornography for him. Pornography may or may not be the type found at an adult bookstore. One man found lingerie ads in newspapers and catalogs to be his form of pornography. Another man found images of large-breasted women to be tantalizing, and he never went further than his everyday TV shows. TP found women with long slender necks stimulating. His subway rides back and forth to work was his pornography studio. In the final analysis, pornography is what each man finds stimulating. What stimulates one man may not stimulate another man. While more classifications of pornography exist, pornography is usually found in the following mediums: literature, photos, Internet, sculptures, drawings, paintings, animation, sound recordings, movies, TV, films, DVDs, Blu-ray, pay-for-view, videos, or video games. Let us look at a few of these.

Literature and photos: The spicy novel with stimulating stories has been around for ages. In the past century, men's magazines such as *Playboy* and *Penthouse* became popular, and the source of initiation into the world of sex for many boys. While these magazines do not violate the Supreme Court's standard of obscenity, adult bookstores sell even more sexually explicit magazines that come close to violating the Supreme Court's standard of obscenity.

Film, DVD, and video: From the midpoint of the previous century, pornography came off the printed page into movement and even more explicit, sexual enactment. Adult bookstores thrived on making available first 8mm movies followed by videocassettes and then DVDs and Blu-rays. Material sold by adult bookstores generally contains hard-core pornography and illicit acts. Adult bookstores look forward to visiting conventioneers who find a trip away from home as an opportunistic time to purchase a future pleasure.

TV and pay-for-view: In recent years, the man who subscribes to a full range of cable or satellite TV channels has available more pornography than he could ever digest. One man said he set his alarm clock for a predawn hour so he could watch stimulating material before going to work. Those who travel frequently may find pay-for-view movies in their hotel room to be their downfall.

Movies: It is difficult to go to a movie theater without being exposed to sexually explicit scenes and nudity. While they are acceptable in today's society, they can cause a man to retain images in his head and mentally process them later, along with masturbation.

Immodest dress: Both women and men dress for attention. Clothing, how it is worn, can be alluring or revealing. Young people may or may not recognize that the way they dress will cause arousal and is very toxic to an addicted man. One man remarked, "I need blinders when I drive across a college campus. Some young women wear less clothing than allowed in a doctor's exam room."

Internet: The Internet is the ultimate presentation of pornography in today's society. While many web sites entice a man to pay for more explicit images, plenty of material is available free. More disturbing is the erotic material that exploits children. If depression was the mental health common cold of the last century, Internet pornography is the pneumonia of this century. Of greater concern is the number of young people and teenagers who have unfettered access to stimulating material on the Internet.

Cybersex: Cybersex has as its common elements the use of a computer, Internet access, expected anonymity, and sexually provocative material to generate arousal followed most often by masturbation. Multiple venues exist such as dial-a-porn, e-mail, chat rooms, live video streams, instant messaging, postings to social networks (like Facebook), visual images of real or graphically generated persons, and interactive sex through a webcam.

Statistics on pornography

The pornography industry is huge and growing. Unfortunately, more children are being exposed to pornography and thus are potential for addiction. The following statistics give insight into just how insidious just one form of stimulation has become—Internet pornography.

Revenue from pornography is more than $97 billion a year. The pornography industry has larger revenues than the revenues of the top technology companies combined: Microsoft, Google, Amazon, eBay, Yahoo, and Apple. Revenue from pornography in the US exceeds the combined revenues of ABC, CBS, and NBC.

- Every second, $3,075.64 is spent on pornography.

- Every second, 28,258 Internet users are viewing pornography.

- Every 39 minutes a new pornographic video is created in the United States

- Every day 68 million pornographic search engine requests are processed --- (25% of search engine requests).

- One hundred thousand web sites offer illegal child pornography.

- The average age of a child's first Internet exposure to pornography is 11.

- Eighty percent of 15-17-year-old teens have had multiple hard-core exposures.

- Ninety percent of 8-16-year-old children have viewed pornography online while doing homework.

- Nearly forty-three percent of adult Internet users view pornography.

- Twenty percent of men admit to accessing pornography at work.

- Forty million US adults regularly visit Internet pornography web sites.

- Fifty-three percent of Promise Keepers viewed pornography in the last week.

- Forty-seven percent of Christians said pornography is a major problem in their homes.

(Family Safe Media, 2012)

The problem that pornography causes in our society are staggering and growing. Just think if while you were at church this past Sunday, you looked left and right, one of the two people you greeted could have said pornography is a problem in their home. If fifty-three percent of Promise Keeper men admit to viewing pornography last week, your partner is far from alone.

Internet pornography content

When one thinks of a man viewing pornography on the Internet, it is reasonable to think of him viewing women in some form of normal sexuality. The reality is the Internet provides both normal as well as a large menu of perverted sexuality. Briefly, examples of perverted sexual behavior are bestiality, sadomasochism (S & M), sexual violence including sadomasochism and rape, exploitation of children, and other perversions that go beyond the need to describe them here.

A therapist asked the members of a group therapy program to disclose the nature of the material they viewed online. The purpose of disclosing pornography content or images was to explore a connection between the addict's current interest and age-inappropriate exposure that occurred during childhood. Identification of such a connection reduces the addictive power of the current pornography content.

Glenn says sexual stimulating material may come from unusual sources.
Glenn was a city boy who was sent to his uncle's farm one summer when he was about the ten years old. To the farm boy, animal copulation is part of everyday business. His cousin realized that Glenn had never seen animals' mate. He took Glenn to the pasture when the veterinarian was on hand to breed a stallion with a prized mare. Glenn was not ready for what he witnessed. He was aroused and confused by seeing the mating process. He remembers dreaming about what saw for a long time. In fact, he became fascinated with human copulation as well.

Glenn, as an adult, stumbled on an Internet site that featured bestiality. He returned to that site and others like it for several years. He never understood why bestiality stimulated him. While in therapy, the connection between what happened at age ten and what kept him fixated as an adult became clear.

If your partner is addicted to Internet pornography, some steps are available to help him and perhaps other members of your family. For those who are not computer savvy, commercial software programs are available to block access to pornography. Type in "blocking software" into the Internet browser search bar, and multiple alternatives will display.

For those who are computer savvy enough to get around Internet blocking programs, software entitled *Covenant Eyes* is an alternative. This software goes beyond blocking access to web sites but also provides a weekly report to a person designated by the user to receive the report. The report details every site the user accessed during the week of reference (covenant eyes, 2012) is available on HTTP: //wwwcovenanteyescom/.

Live the life you've dreamed
David Henry Thoreau

Chapter Ten

The Recovery

Journey

The books found on the Amazon website (under Paul Becker, LPC) guide the man who wishes to overcome sexual addiction. An overview of the information found in the Recovery Guide is presented here to give insight concerning issues your partner may wish to address in therapy.

- **Acknowledging the problem**

Recovery begins with acknowledging the problem. For many, acknowledging the problem is not as simple as it sounds. Frequently, a man enters therapy to placate a partner's outrage after her partner's aberrant sexual behaviors has been discovered. Agreeing to go to therapy may not be a commitment to change behavior. Denial of the seriousness of the problem and thus, the need for a solution is common. Usually, if the man remains in therapy, he overcomes denial and begins a true recovery process.

Your job is asking your partner to consider making to long-term commitment. His commitment will occur during therapy and while attending frequent Twelve Step will hear that he is neither alone in his addiction nor as evil as he fears.

- **Awareness leads to choices**

A therapist can almost see the addict's awareness light bulb go on. When the addict begins to understand that behavior is causing significant pain to himself and his family, enlightenment has begun.

Ultimately, he will face a choice to change his lifestyle and curtail his aberrant sexual behavior. Interestingly, long-term recovery is not just a matter of ending behavior; it is a matter of changing both internal and external environments so that the adverse behavioral breeding ground is decimated.

Ending sexual thinking and fantasy is an example of changing the addict's internal environment. Sexual sobriety cannot be maintained unless the brain is inspired to end tantalizing erotic images.

An example of an external environmental change is eliminating the addict's chronically depressed mood. This is not simply saying, "I am a happy person." It means initiating and maintaining positive behaviors that foster a new outlook on life. It means choosing activities that foster living at the forty-point benchmark level. When a man chooses to live at the forty-point benchmark level, as discussed in Chapter 7, he seeks uplifting scenarios such as daily exercise, frequent dates with his partner, a supportive male friend, and other activities that improve his relationships with his immediate and extended family. Living at the forty-point benchmark level diminishes chronically depressed mood and lowers the propensity to act-out.

These examples are, but some of the sobriety steps your partner will want to pursue if he is committed to changing the addiction dance.

- **Commitment**

In humor, a smoker might say, "I am committed to stopping every time I put a cigarette out. I've done it thousands of times." For the addict, the same phrase is not humorous. The addict has committed to himself to quit many times. The reason why the addict is unable to maintain his commitment is that his internal and external environments have not changed. For example, internally, he has not freed himself from sexual thinking and fantasy. Externally he has not freed himself from isolation and low-grade depression.

The addict continues to struggle with temptations because he allows the temptation to bounce around in his brain. The man continues to "white knuckle" his addiction. When temptation comes, he struggles (white knuckle) to rid himself of temptation, but then he succumbs to temptation, repeatedly. As long as he continues to "white knuckle," his recovery will be problematical.

An alternative to "white knuckling" is making a "high-level commitment." The difference between "white knuckling" and "high-level commitment" is the approach to the decision. In a "white knuckling" approach, he or she does not eliminate the possibility of succumbing to temptation. As an example, when one who likes to view pornography tells him or herself I will no longer look at pornographic magazines but does not destroy all the porn collection, it's called "white knuckling" one's commitment. Hidden away are several choice magazines against the day one needs a fix. If the whole collection was eliminated and other sources of pornography (pornographic movies, CDs, and provocative cable channels, etc.) thus rejecting the source of temptation, an important step has been taken toward sexual sobriety. A addict who makes a "high-level commitment" totally rejects the possibility of acting out.

It is not easy to explain what a "high-level commitment" looks like as contrasted to "white knuckling." Full understanding comes only with experiencing a "high-level commitment." It is only after the addict commits to eliminate all acting-out behavior and does so, that he gains an experiential understanding. Once he experiences a "high-level commitment," the impact of temptation changes. When a man "white knuckles' his recovery, he continually struggles to reject a temptation, but often fails. When the addict lives a "high-level commitment," the struggle ends. Since one is totally committed to rejecting acting-out, the temptation is neutralized at its inception.

- **Recognition that addiction causes more pain than pleasure**

Sexual stimulation leads to orgasm. The "rush" experienced during orgasm is as God intended, pleasurable. The time needed to act out is relatively short. Eventually, a recovering addict realizes time spent acting out as contrasted to time spent in shame and guilt is out of balance. This can be a decision point for the addict. The addict may realize that acting out is not worth the consequences, that is, extended time of feeling shame, guilt, isolation, anger, procrastination, and depression.

Addicts ultimately realize it is impossible to be intimate with self (self-sex) and intimate in the marriage with the same intensity. Addicts report that arousal and orgasm with self are more intense because the addict is in control of the entire scenario. He needs no one's cooperation but himself. However, marital sex is relational, and in the long run, far more satisfying. Marital relations carry no sense of shame or guilt.

How can sex be pleasurable and, at the same time, cause pain? The addict likes the feeling he experiences during orgasm. He or she enjoys the euphoric feeling associated with orgasm, and repeats acting-out behavior to duplicate that feeling.

However, for many, the euphoric feeling is followed by prolonged feelings of remorse. Such feelings remain until the acting-out cycle begins again. Since he or she has not experienced the joy of long-term sobriety, they lack understanding. An addict simply no longer knows what the alternative to acting out looks like. For the addict, acting out is his normal. A competent therapist can help the addict see reality; "I am experiencing more pain than pleasure." A man in therapy said, "Why am I doing this to myself?"

In therapy, the addict begins to understand, despite the pleasure of self-stimulation, his or her behavior is selfish, often child-like, and always shameful. One begins to understand that one's behavior ultimately causes more pain to self. Those who have spent many years in prison fear to get out because they do not know if they can adjust. Your partner has spent many years in the prison of sexual addiction. He, too, does not know what it will be like to live on the other side of addiction. An often heard comment in therapy is, "I don't know what it's like not to be sexually addicted. I don't know what normal looks like."

When a man or woman in therapy begins to talk about how much pain addiction is causing, relative to the short periods of pleasure, another light bulb goes on. This enlightenment is a significant milestone in his recovery.

During therapy, your partner should gain insight and experience a series of "light bulb" moments. Each one will bring him or her closer to making a high-level commitment. If your partner is committed he can share in insights and the joy of recovery. It is critical to his recovery and the health of your relationship that you care.

Modifying the environment

We have noted several times that a critical step in the addict's recovery is to maintain a commitment to change internal and external environments. Without going into detail, a sexually addicted man will need to address: Install blocking software on his computer.

Eliminate pay-for-view stimulating channels. Learn to "bounce one's eyes" (The term "bouncing eyes" was popularized by Arterburn to mean a man needs to look away when he encounters a stimulating image or person) (Arterburn, 2000).

- Learn to change the channel when a provocative show is on the TV. Say "no" to pornography found in magazines, DVDs and Blu-ray videos, ads in newspapers, the Internet, etc.

- Say "no" to participation in chat rooms, phone sex, massage parlors, strip joints, lap dancing, etc.

- Get rid of "stash," (Stash is material kept in secret for the day when the addict believes he needs a reward).
- Learn to focus on a woman's face rather than her "body parts."
- Understand each woman (even a porn star) is somebody's mother, sister, daughter, or spouse.
  These are examples of tools one can address in recovery. Each addict has stimulating triggers. Part of the recovery journey requires him or her to make a rigorous inventory of that which begins one's acting-out ritual. (Addressed needs will differ from one to another).

An addict may identify something he finds stimulating that society would not consider sexual. For example, in therapy a man disclosed that pictures of sailboats with cabins are stimulating, but he had no idea why. He learned that the connection between stimulating images of a sailboat came from the sexual abuse he experienced while on a sailboat as a child. Each time he saw a sailboat, his child within responded with arousal to the abuse he experienced. For him, once he understood the connection, it lessened the power of the stimulus. However, it was also helpful to stay away from pictures of sailboats with cabins, at least early in his recovery journey.

- **Choosing a healthy lifestyle**

  A link between a chronically depressed mood and acting out is interesting. To reduce the disparity of living at the twenty-point benchmark and acting out at the fifty-point benchmark, a conscious decision must be made to incorporate more forty-point activities into one's life. Some of the activities may include:

- A weekly exercise program sufficient to achieve an "endorphin high." While an "endorphin high" is not as powerful as the high associated with orgasm, it does have legitimate substitution value.

- Incorporate healthy activities into one's life, such as hiking, biking, softball, tennis, golf, soccer, etc. (Ideally, some of these healthy activities will be family or couple activities.)
- Participate in a weekly mood-lifting activity with one's partner and or family.
- Develop a healthy relationship with a higher power or God. It is a blessing for the addict to realize God is his greatest cheerleader. God blesses his struggle; he does not condemn failures.
- Volunteer to help others. A spiritual connection is tied to serving others. When the focus is switched from self to others, the vision of the world in changes. Addicts are takers. Long term healing occurs when they become givers. Any new and positive behavior one chooses to raise mood in a healthy way.

- **Come out of isolation**

  The addict lives in a world where his focus is internal. Addicts are self-centered and fulfilling their needs come first. Isolation is often a consequence of low-grade depression. Some of the activities a man will find helpful to address "come out of isolation" include:

- **Cultivate a strong male relationship.**

  Because an addict lives in shame, he or she find it a challenge to let anyone get close to his or her secrets. A healthy relationship with another male is part of the recovery plan. Such a relationship serves to break the shame-based isolation that characterizes life. The goal is to trust another male so both can share their struggles and secrets. A place to look for a healthy male relationship is in a Twelve-step program, church group, and a therapy group.

- **Improve relationships with the family of origin.**

  Since addicts are the product of dysfunctional families, relationships between parents and siblings are often damaged. Such damage leads to isolation. When the addict begins to understand that siblings, as well as parents, carry the wounds of generational family shame, he can show empathy and foster bonding with them. Addicts are encouraged to approach parents and siblings with the question, "What was it like for you to grow up in our/your family of origin?" This question is an icebreaker and non-threatening. Although it may take time, opening a dialogue with siblings and parents is therapeutic and heals the past.

- **Improve relationships with a partner and children.**

  A man experiences more intimacy outside the marriage than he does with his partner and children. For him, intimacy equals sex. He has no concept of non-sexual intimacy. In fact, it is quite common to learn that during their courting relationship, the addict and future partner included sexual activity. Once sexual activity entered their relationship, the process of building friendship ended. The focus was on obtaining more sex. Improving the relationship with his partner requires a commitment to change the dynamics of their marriage. Both need to invest in non-sexual intimacy daily. Examples of non-sexual intimacy are taking a walk or going to the gym or reading a book or making dinner together.

- **Abstain from marital relations**

  The couple time to form a friendship that was a missing ingredient during courtship. That means spending time talking, sharing non-sexual activities, sharing meals, a weekly date, and just about any other activity that builds friendship in the marriage. Most couples report joy when their partner becomes their best friend. When both marriage partners can say "yes" too many of the statements below, isolation in the marriage has dissipated.

  I know that I have intimacy in my marriage when:
  - I consider my partner to be a very good listener.
  - My partner understands how I feel.
  - We have a good balance of leisure time spent together and separately.
  - I look forward to spending time with my partner.
  - We find it easy to think of activities to do together.
  - I am very satisfied with how we talk to each other.
  - We always try to do something nice for each other (without looking for thanks).
  - We are creative in how we handle our differences.
  - Making joint financial decisions is not difficult.
  - We are both equally willing to adjust our relationship.
  - I can share feelings and ideas with my partner during disagreements.
  - My partner understands my opinions and ideas.
  - My partner is my best friend.
  - My partner does not try to fix me. We agree it is my job to fix me.

Likewise, the man often has a shallow relationship with his children. Sharing time with children, and knowing them as precious human beings, changes the dynamic of isolation in the family.

Recovery is not a passive sport

Addictive behavior will not end by just attending therapy, Twelve Step meetings, and prayer. The addict must formulate a plan to change his or her lifestyle, avoid environmental triggers, and commit to change his or her environment.

As the man's partner or significant other, your understanding and support is part of the man's program. Be willing to listen but do not act as his therapist or accountability partner. Listening is very powerful. It is a true act of love. Also, this is an ideal time for both of you to grow in wisdom by attending self-help groups or participating in one's own therapy.

Multiple layers of acting-out behavior

Rarely does an addict end all addictive behaviors at one time. Giving up sexual behaviors is often done in stages or layers.

The first layer is overt sexual behavior that the addict believes society rejects. For example, ending massage parlors, soliciting prostitutes, engaging in voyeurism, pursuing extra-marital affairs, and participating in other egregious behaviors is easier to give up than pornography and masturbation.

The second layer is private behavior unacceptable at the workplace. Pornography on the Internet is a prime example. Most consider, contrary to the reality, that the Internet is a private place. **It is not!** Ask a man who lost his job because his employer discovered his use of pornography in the workplace.

Many believe the internet is a private space. **It is not!** The private space is more like a fishbowl. For multiple reasons, IP address are maintained to answer law enforcement queries and maintaining data bases has become a prime industry money maker.

The next layer is pornography on the home computer. While the draw to find more sensuous images will likely continue, a man finally realizes that pornography and masturbation are as toxic as any acting-out behavior. Again, private space on one's computer is more like working in a fishbowl.

The last layer is sexual prism. Addiction is more than overt behavior. At the core is brain activity. An addict engages in erotic thinking and fantasies daily. The addict sees the world through a sexual prism. For example, when he opens a magazine, he views the images through his sexual prism. If his fetish is women with large breasts, he will check each image against his internal standard. Virtually everything in his world and every image is processed through his prism. A man who has given up physically acting-out may still have an active prism. A man who has given up pornography and masturbation may still engage in sexual thinking and fantasy.

Giving up his thinking, fantasy, and one's prism is your partner's greatest challenge. He has processed images unconsciously for their sexual content for years, going back into childhood. To be able to pick up a magazine or to watch TV without dwelling on body parts requires a very high-level commitment. For most men it will take years for him to work through this layer. The temptation is life-long.

What needs to change is his ability to reject temptation in the present moment. As in time he invests in sexual sobriety, he will no longer experience the pain of acting out. The addict eventually will reject physical behaviors in addition to his sexual prism.

Therapy

It is common to hear one say, "I don't need therapy; all I have to do is try harder and pray more." He may believe he has his problem under control after a short period of sobriety. Likely, he is in denial of the seriousness of one's problem The nature of compulsivity is the lack of control over one's behavior. The answer lies in changing one's lifestyle to address the underlying reasons for addiction. A trained therapist is in the best position to help your partner begin his life-changing journey.

In addition to individual therapy, group therapy is a powerful tool to help an addicted man or woman to begin to shed the shame of aberrant sexual behavior. Group therapy helps a one work through shame and fears. A great fear is how he or she will cope when it comes time to give up the addict's best friend—addiction. In a group setting a man hears other addict's stories, which serve to enlighten and provide hope to each participant.

An essential component of the recovery journey is participation in a Twelve Step program. A trained therapist facilitates individual and group therapy; Twelve Step programs are peer administered. Twelve Step programs have important tasks:

- Benefit from strength. Provide a forum for men and women to talk about their struggle with a common demon and to gather strength from each other.

- Break isolation. Members connect through sharing strengths, hopes, and experiences.

- Foster a learning forum. Personal stories reveal that others think, feel, and behave in similar ways.

- Gather support. Members divulge unhealthy behaviors and grow into healthy, caring adults who support each other's growth.

- Foster sobriety. Group accountability is a motivator for achieving sobriety. An adjunct to Twelve-step meetings are sponsors or accountability partners. They are available for frequent contact, encouragement, and accountability. They provide a recovery context for working through the Twelve Steps. The Twelve Step programs are time tested and allow the sexually addicted to continue one's recovery journey into the future, long after therapy has ended.

What can a woman do?

After discovering your partner's acting-out, you may wish to consider.

- Insist your partner enter sexual addiction therapy. For your partner's benefit it may be desirable to add a consequence if he does not seek help. (If this is codependent behavior, so be it! This condition is for your health and sanity.)

- Focus on your recovery. Attend support group programs or engage in individual therapy. Support groups for partners, or significant others, provide information about addiction and boundaries that are important to individual and marital growth. They also provide relationships with other women who are in similar circumstances. During your worst nightmare, it is important to know you are not alone.

- Read books on addiction to gain more insight into this addiction.

- Examine how codependency has governed your marriage relationship. Identify changes you wish to make. Do this with the help of a therapist who can guide you through the underlying factors that foster codependency.

- Keep the relationship with your partner civil. Do not make decisions with long-term consequences currently. Be available to listen to your partner's newly gained insights from therapy. Do not play the role of his therapist; just listen.

- Foster non-sexual friendship. Engage in multiple weekly forty-point benchmark activities with your partner.

- Addiction devastates trust and dreams. It may not be possible to recreate old dreams, but it is essential to formulate new-shared dreams. Ultimately, marital therapy is part of the recovery journey.

A marriage based on full confidence, based on complete and unqualified frankness on both sides; they are not keeping anything back; there's no deception underneath it all. If I might so put it, it's an agreement for the

mutual forgiveness of sin.

Henrik Ibs

Chapter Eleven

Putting it all Together

You have uncovered considerable new material. It may be challenging to understand all the various concepts. Although you are enlightened as to the nature of addiction, you may still feel dismayed. The recovery task is strenuous for your partner as well as the rest of the family. Perhaps two more stories will present how two high profile people experienced addiction and subsequently progressed to healing and recovery.

Dr. Mark Laaser, Debbie Laaser (Mark's spouse), Dr. Patrick Carnes, and Marnie C. Ferree appeared on Dateline on February 22, 2004, to tell their *Sex Addiction Stories.*

Dr. Laaser and Marnie Ferree shared how sex addiction took over their lives. The following stories are from an article by Keith Morrison (2004), *Battling Sex Addiction,* and is based on the Dateline program. See if you can pick out the characteristics of addiction common to your partner's experience. A checklist follows the stories.

Mark and Debbie's Laaser

Mark is Rev. Dr. Mark Laaser. According to his web site, Mark Laaser is an internationally known author and speaker. His first book, *Faithful and True,* was the first Christian book to address the issue of addiction. He has since written six other books including, *Talking to Your Kids About Sex,* and his most recent, *The Pornography Trap* (with Dr. Ralph Earle). Dr. Laaser has counseled hundreds of sex addicts and their families, consulted with numerous churches, developed treatment programs for a variety of hospitals, and has conducted workshops and seminars worldwide.

Dr. Laaser currently serves as director of the Institute for Healthy Sexuality of the American Association of Christian Counselors, and as executive director of Faithful and True Ministries. Dr. Laaser holds a Ph.D. in Religion and Psychology from the University of Iowa, a Master of Divinity from Princeton Theological Seminary, and a bachelor's degree in Religion and Philosophy from Augustana College in Rock Island, Illinois. He currently resides in Minnesota with his wife, Debbie. They have three grown children: Sarah, Jonathan, and Benjamin. Laaser, M (2012).

Debbie Laaser holds her MA in Marriage and Family Therapy from the Alder Graduate School. She works with her husband, Mark, to provide support for women and counseling couples at their counseling center. She authored *Shattered Vows* and was the co-author with Mark of *The Seven Desires of Every Heart.* Laaser, D (2012).

Now Mark and Debbie's story:

There was that selfish needy, lonely, angry part of myself that didn't want to stop and saw that sex was my solution to other things, says Mark. He seemed to have an insatiable need for secret sex. To anyone who knew him, it would have seemed incomprehensible. Although married with children, a minister, and counselor, an icon of respect, it was not enough. Mark says, early on, he felt an emptiness, a loneliness that sex seemed to fill.

It was just excitement, a raw excitement—kind of like what a drug addict would describe, says Mark. It was just a high.
It was a high Mark began to experience at a young age.
When he was 11, he discovered pictures, what we would call soft porn now. And some of that is not abnormal for a person seeing that for the first time. Of course, when it becomes abnormal is how preoccupied you get with it. Then for me, I started crossing moral boundaries almost right away. Stealing magazines—and I am a preacher's kid, a minister's son. So, I knew that stealing was bad. But I was willing to go ahead with it because the high I was experiencing was so fantastic.

In high school, Mark hoped his behavior might stop when he met Debbie, the girl he thought could change him

> There was a part of myself that she just didn't know
> because I wasn't revealing it to her or anybody for that
> matter.

Mark wasn't revealing that he was now doing more than looking at magazines. He was watching porn videos and masturbating daily. Debbie, unaware of Mark's double life, trusted him and they got married. Mark hoped that married life would end a life pre-occupied by sex. All this crazy stuff in the past...will be over now.

I'm getting married. I'll have a regular sexual partner and so forth, he reasoned. But I was amazed early on, even in the first year of

marriage, that my temptation to masturbate and look at pornography returned rather quickly. Many people think human beings are preoccupied with sex, so what would be so unusual?

The unusual part was where my mind tended to go with it, says Mark. I wanted to experience it. I wanted to act it out. Eventually, I had a lot of preoccupation with planning or doing or thinking about what it would be like.

Mark soon was no longer planning, but doing, paying monthly visits to massage parlors, having sex with so-called "masseuses," all the while hiding it from Debbie,

I was always completely attracted to her. There was just something so much deeper in me that cannot be satisfied by sex.

He says something deeply emotional was missing, and he wondered why he did not just stop. Probably a million times throughout my acting-out history.

Mark was building toward behavior he would never have thought possible for him. He had degrees in religion and divinity, had attended seminary school, and was a deeply committed Christian who by this time was an ordained minister.

There was that good side. There was that moral side. There was that caring side. Yet, he would escape, furtive and guilty, to feed his addiction. At the same time, he was working on getting his Ph.D. in, of all things, psychology.

Now I'm the Reverend Dr. Laaser. Also, some people are going to be attracted to that, and I actually wound up becoming sexual with some of my clients at that time. It happened multiple times over 10-years. [I was] frightened, incredibly frightened. I think for years, I felt worthless. I can't describe to you the times I would sit in church, even preaching on a Sunday morning, thinking God's grace was for everybody else but certainly not for me.

Mark was preaching redemption, but for him, redemption might be more difficult. He betrayed parishioners, colleagues, and clients. It was a trust about to be shattered.

> One of the people I was involved in had reported that—yes, the very thing I was afraid of happened.

Eight very angry people called me in, canceled my appointments for that day. He says he did not even realize what they knew until the first one opened his mouth and started talking. Then it all came crashing in on me. His colleagues at the center angrily confronted and fired him. They would help him get treatment for his sexual misbehavior, but first, they said, he had to tell his wife Debbie, everything.

I was totally blind sided, says Debbie. I had no idea that this man I had been living with for 15 years—married to for 15 years—could have been doing all these things. Also, I will never forget the look on Mark's face. He was sitting in a chair across from me, and I guess today what I know is broken-ness in a person. I think there were times truthfully when I questioned whether I would stay. There were times I know when I felt so extremely sad that I wasn't sure we would ever be able to have happiness in our life again.

Then amid all that pain, her husband felt something else.

This pent up secret that is now over 30 years old is now suddenly out of the bag. I do not have to protect the secret anymore. So, I think I mixed up with fear, sadness, and confusion there was a sense of relief.

He has been in recovery for over a decade. He says it is a continuing process. After his sexual misbehavior was exposed, Mark entered a sex addiction treatment center for a month, where he received psychotherapy called Faithful and True Ministries. He still occasionally goes for counseling and relies on the support of those around him—like Debbie—who stayed by his side through it all.

I never had these real feelings of just running and leaving, says Debbie. I wasn't aware that running would solve anything necessarily.

Their relationship eventually strengthened. They dealt with some of the loneliness Mark felt and both found comfort in their religious faith.

Now that Debbie and I are more spiritually intimate, sex in our relationship is satisfying, says Mark.

His work has also helped him. He is again counseling others—including men with problems like his.

Marnie's C. Ferree

Marnie C. Ferree is a licensed marriage and family therapist employed with the Woodmont Hills Church in Nashville, Tennessee, which is the sponsoring organization for Bethesda Workshops. She has a national reputation as a leader in the field of addiction, particularly as it presents in women. In 1997, Marnie established a workshop program for female sex addicts that was the first of its kind in the country and today draws participants from across the United States and Canada. She has directed Bethesda Workshops since 2000. Previously, Marnie provided counseling for recovery (both from sexual abuse and sexual addiction) through the Woodmont Hills Counseling Center, a sister ministry at the church. Marnie is a frequent lecturer at professional and recovery conferences, churches, and schools. She also consults with Christian organizations and churches about sexual integrity, especially in cases where a leader has fallen into sexual sin.

Marnie's book about female sexual addiction, *No Stones: Women Redeemed from Sexual Shame,* is the first Christian book on the subject by a woman personally in recovery. *No Stones* has been widely acclaimed as a pioneering work and is considered the standard in the field. Her second book is "*L.I.F.E. Guide for Women,*" a workbook for female sex addicts.

Marnie and her husband David have been married since 1981 and are parents of a young adult son, married daughter, and grandparents of an infant grandson. (Ferree, 2012).

Now Marnie's story:

(Except for some minor changes, the following text is the words of Keith Morrison)

I was wracked with shame and tried time and time again to stop,
says Marnie.

Like Mark, she knows what it is like to be out of control. For Marnie, it
was not so much about sex itself, but about the relationships, she
thought she could have by engaging in sex with acquaintances and
friends.

The sexual part was pleasurable, and it was a nice, but that wasn't
the most important thing. I was trying to get non-sexual needs
met sexually, and that was the only way I knew how to meet
those needs.

As a child, Marnie was sexually abused by a family friend, a common
precursor to later addiction. Her promiscuity lasted from her teen years
through two marriages, with numerous affairs. She felt an emotional void
she says that sex filled—at least initially.

At the time, there is an incredible adrenaline rush. It is a
connection that I found could not replicate anywhere else. But
immediately after that experience is over, I mean driving back
home, there is this incredible letdown, and you're just in the wash
of shame.

That shame worsened after Marnie was diagnosed with cervical cancer.
The cause, she was told, was a sexually transmitted disease.

That was the lowest point I experienced; three surgeries in a year
as a treatment for cervical cancer. I had a major hemorrhaging
after one of those surgeries. I mean my life was literally in danger,
and still, I found I could not stop.

191

She was sick, married, a mother, and yet none of those things could make her change, even though she was horrified by what she was doing.

> It's about feeling rotten; I want to feel better. What way am I going through a ritual to feel better? I am connecting with someone; I am going to act out sexually. I feel horrible after that, and the whole cycle starts over again.

Marnie was desperate. Sex with her husband was not enough, and she believed the only way to stop having sex outside her marriage, was to end her life.

> I had strong suicidal thoughts. But I knew I couldn't keep on living, but I was too afraid to die. I've sometimes gone home with people I'm not even that attracted to, and yet I feel like if I don't have sex with them; it's just the most horrible feeling.

Marnie thought sex was her solution to painful feelings. However, the solution was not working.

After years of failing to stop having sex with acquaintances, she was ready to take her own life. Then, at last, she confided in someone. I picked up the phone and called a dear friend and poured out this awful saga of my life and said I need help.

She did get help. A therapist helped her learn to deal with the childhood sexual abuse that contributed to her many affairs. Her second marriage survived and is, she says, better. She was surprised to find she was not alone.

About a third of sex addicts are female, which is why to do something to help other women, she went back to school to get a degree in counseling.

> I didn't choose sex addiction. Sex addiction chose me, and this field chose me. Women are afraid to talk about it. We are afraid of being labeled as whores. It is guys will be guys; men will be men. But for a woman to be out of control in her sexual behavior, there is just a whole other level of shame.

What did you find in these stories?

Dr. Mark Laaser, Debbie Laaser (Mark's spouse), and Marnie Ferree showed courage in sharing their stories on Dateline. They provide a broad spectrum of characteristics found in addiction. Your challenge is to listen to their stories and affirm hearing any of the following characteristics:

- The power of addiction is compulsive.
- Secret sex is an addiction.
- Addiction often begins in childhood.
- The expectation that marriage would end the temptation to act out is false.
- Addicts are preoccupied with planning their acting-out ritual.
- Addicts hide behind the mask of respectability and lead a dual life.
- Addiction has a profound impact on one's relationship with God.
  Denial is nearly universal.
  An out of control life is a product of addiction.
- As children, many addicts are abused.
- Shame is a consequence of acting out.
- Addicts tend to be blind to the consequences of acting out.
- One's acting-out cycle is repeated over and over.
- Medicating pain is an excuse for acting out.

- Addiction for a woman is often based on relationship expectations.
- Suicidal thoughts compound shame for the addict.
- Disclosing secrets is an early recovery task.
- A decision to change is a high-level commitment.
- Unmanageability describes acting-out behavior
- A new outcome accompanies recovery.

Summary

For the wife or significant other, the task of dealing with an impaired partner in the open for the first time can be overwhelming. Remember, your partner did not become addicted overnight, and he will not become sober overnight. Both Bradshaw and Carnes believe that the recovery journey takes years (Carnes, 1991, Bradshaw, 1988)

An important question for many women is: should I stay, or should I leave my partner? Unfortunately, the answer is not a simple yes or no. As Dr. Mark Laaser witnessed, his wife, Debbie, stayed with him. The recovery has fostered a new sense of life for both. On the other hand, Marnie Ferrer's first husband did not stay with her. At the time of her divorce from her first husband, she was not ready for an addiction-free relationship.

A tenet of marriage therapy is for the partners to solve their relationship weaknesses in their present environment. If they do not, they will repeat the same problems in their next relationship. While you did not cause your partner's addictive behavior, your personality type, and the wounds, you suffered while maturing contributed to the dynamics of the marriage. In marriages that include an addicted man, the partner is advised to enter therapy to address her own issues. Generally, therapy is not complete until the couple participates in marriage therapy. Overcoming codependency in the marriage is also a key to long-term recovery.

Appendix A

Unwanted Sexual Behaviors
Found in the DSM-V

The bible of mental health definitions for counselors and therapists is the *Diagnostic and Statistical Manual of Mental Disorders, DSM V.* The *DSM V* satisfies the need to classify mental disorders, to agree on common definitions, to offer diagnostic assistance to mental health specialists, to codify insurance processing, and to carry out statistical analysis. It is the product of much research and study and represents the American Psychiatric Association's guide to the mental health community at large.

The *DSM V* classifies only a small proportion of what is considered aberrant sexual behaviors. Nevertheless, it is a good place to start. *DSM V* defines unwanted sexual behaviors as paraphilia's (American Psychiatric Association, 2000). All paraphilia's, according to the *DSM V*, is characterized by reoccurring, intense sexual urges, sexual fantasies, or behaviors. Such fantasies, sexual urges, or behaviors must occur over at least six months. They must also cause significant stress or impair one's social, occupational, or everyday functioning for a diagnosis to be made. There is also a sense of distress within these individuals. Typically, one recognizes the symptoms as negatively influencing their lives but believes they are unable to control them.
Paraphilias included in the *DSM-V* are:

- **Exhibitionism** involves the surprise exposure of one's genitals to a stranger. Exposure may coincide with masturbation and a fantasy expectation that the stranger will become sexually aroused.

-

-

- **Fetishism** involves the use of nonliving objects, for example, a woman's undergarments, or other worn apparel, to achieve a state of arousal. The man frequently masturbates while holding, rubbing, or smelling the apparel. He may ask his partner to wear apparel during intercourse. The fetish is either preferred or required for sexual excitement.

- **Frotteurism** involves touching and rubbing one's genitals against a non-consenting person. The behavior generally occurs in crowded places to avoid arrest. The behavior may also involve fondling. During the act, the person usually fantasizes an exclusive, caring relationship with the victim.

- **Pedophilia** is characterized by sexual activity with a child, usually age 13 or younger, or in the case of an adolescent, a child five years younger than the pedophile.

- **Masochism** involves the act of being humiliated, beaten, bound, or otherwise made to suffer to enhance or achieve sexual excitement. In some cases, the act is limited to a fantasy of being raped while being held or bound by others so that there is no possibility of escape. Sexual Masochism may involve a wide range of devices to achieve the desired effect, including some that may cause death.

- **Sadism** involves an act in which the individual derives sexual excitement from the psychological or physical suffering, including the humiliation of the victim. The partner may or may not be consenting. Sadism may involve a range of behaviors and devices to achieve the desired effect.

- **Transvestic fetishism** involves heterosexual males who dress in female clothes (cross-dressing) to produce or enhance sexual arousal, usually without a real partner, but with the fantasy that they are the female partner. Women's garments are arousing primarily as symbols of the individual's femininity.

- **Voyeurism** involves observing an unknowing and non-consenting person, usually a stranger, who is naked or in the process of becoming unclothed and engaging in sexual activity. The act of looking (peeping) is intended to produce sexual excitement and is usually accompanied by self-masturbation. Fantasies from such acts are used to fuel future masturbation.

Unwanted Sexual Behaviors NOT Found in DSM-V

The following unwanted sexual behaviors are not included in the *DSM-V* but may result in significant stress or impair one's social, occupational, or everyday functioning.

- **Extra-marital affairs** involve single or multiple sexual relationships with partners outside the marriage that cause significant stress to the marriage relationship. Men often justify an affair because of a perception of unfulfilled expectations within the marriage. Swinging and wife swapping are aberrant forms of extramarital affairs that include the participation of both partners in the marriage.

- **Multiple or anonymous partners** often involve homosexual relationships— frequently anonymous, situational, and intended to provide sexual experience. Homosexual encounters also may be habitual since they are repeated with new partners. They are particularly dangerous to the parties if practiced without the protection of a condom because participants are exposed to venereal disease and/or HIV.

- **Prostitution** involves the solicitation and procurement of various types of sexual behavior from male or female escorts or prostitutes.

- **Sexual massage** involves the solicitation and procurement of sex, most often, oral sex or masturbation, from a male or female who provides massages. In most cases, those who seek such services engage in other aberrant sexual behaviors.

- Sexual anorexia involves an obsessive state in which the physical, mental, and emotional tasks of avoiding sex dominates one's life. Preoccupation with the avoidance of sex may be used to mask or avoid one's life problems. The obsession can then become a way to cope with all stress and all life difficulties.

Compulsive sexual behaviors

Our society judges some sexual behaviors as reasonably normal. Among men, little stigma is attached to them. The concepts "every male does it," "it doesn't hurt anyone," or similar thinking is used to justify the behavior. What changes a behavior from acceptable to unacceptable is compulsivity, that is, it is engaged excessively; becomes time consuming; interferes with a person's daily routine, work, or social functioning; continues despite no longer being pleasurable or gratifying; places the individual at risk of physical harm; or has legal or personal consequences and leads to financial debt. Examples include:

- **Masturbation** involves sexual self-stimulation, most commonly by touching, stroking, or massaging the penis, clitoris, or vagina until orgasm is achieved. Masturbation is the most common form of sexual behavior.

- **Pornography** is any material that depicts or describes a sexual function for stimulating sexual arousal upon the part of the consumer.

- **Cybersex** has as its common elements the use of a computer, Internet access, expected anonymity, and sexually provocative material to generate arousal followed most often by masturbation. Behaviors include visual images of real or graphics generated persons, interactive sex through a webcam, chat rooms, and e-mail. Cybersex is increasing at a high rate.

- **Phone Sex** has as its common element the use of a phone to talk or listen to a provocative repertoire to generate arousal followed, most often, by masturbation.

Appendix B

Supplemental Reading

Books by Dr. Patrick Carnes

The Betrayal Bond: Breaking Free of Exploitive Relationships,
This book presents an in-depth study of exploitive relationships: why they form, who is most susceptible, and how they become so powerful. It explains how to recognize when traumatic bonding has occurred.

Facing the Shadow: Starting Sexual and Relationship Recovery (3rd edition12-1-150
This workbook helps the addict work through denial, understanding the addictive cycle, and identifying compulsive behaviors.

A Gentle Path through the 12 Steps.
This book provides exercises, inventories, and guided reflections for those who face the daily challenge of maintaining an addiction-free lifestyle.

Don't Call It Love: Recovery from Sexual Addiction.
This book is based on the testimony of more than one thousand recovering sex addicts in the first major scientific study of the disorder.

Out of the Shadows: Understanding Sexual Addiction, (rev 3rd ed.)

This book is the first to describe sexual addiction. It is the standard for recognizing and overcoming this destructive sexual behavior.

The Betrayal Bond: Breaking Free of Exploitive Relationships
This book addresses dysfunctional relationships.

In the Shadows of the Net: Breaking Free of Compulsive Online Sexual Behavior, by Carnes, P, Delmonico, D & Griffi N, E. (2001).
The book provides an Internet Screening Test to help people decide if they have a problem with their use of sexual material on the Internet.

Other readings

Cybersex Unhooked: A Workbook for Breaking Free of Compulsive Online Sexual Behavior, by David Delmonico D, Griffin, E, and Moriarity, J (2001).
Helps people understand cybersex behaviors and provides concrete exercises to help them break free from compulsive online sexual behavior.

Every Man's Battle: Winning the War on Sexual Temptation, One Victory at a Time, by Arterburn, S, Stoeker, F, & Yorkey, M (2000).
The authors examine the challenge every man faces—sexual temptation. The book denies the perception men are unable to control their thought, lives, and roving eyes.

Bradshaw on: The Family, by Bradshaw, J (1988).
Focus is on the dynamics of the family; how the rules and attitudes learned while growing up become encoded within each family member.

Disclosing Secrets: When, to Whom and How Much to Reveal, by Corley, D, & Schneider, J (2002).

A guide to revealing sexual addiction secrets to one's partner and others.

Mending a Shattered Heart—A Guide for Partners of Sex Addicts, by Carnes, S (ed) (2008).

For the partner who needs an answer to the question: Where do I go from here?

Getting the Love, You Want: A Guide for Couples, millennium edition (rep ed) Hendrix, H (2001).

Presents relationship skills to help couples replace confrontation and criticism with a healing process of mutual growth and support. It describes the techniques of Imago Relationship Therapy.

Healing the Wounds of Sexual Addiction, by Laaser, M (20014).

Offers help and hope for regaining and maintaining sexual integrity, self-control, and wholesome, biblical sexuality.

Back from Betrayal: Recovering from His Affairs, (2nd ed) by Schneider, J (2001).

Provides practical help for women involved with sex-addicted men.

Untangling the Web: Sex, Porn and Fantasy Obsession, by Weiss, D and Schneider, J (2006).

Provides offers healing strategies for anyone experiencing the negative impact of Internet pornography and sex addiction.

Women, Sex, and Addiction: A Search for Love and Power, by Kasl, C (1990). Guides women through an understanding of addiction and sexual codependency. It leads women to recovery.

Sex Lies and Forgiveness: Couples Speaking Out on Healing from Sex Addiction by Schneider, B., & Schneider, J. (2004). (3rd ed.). Recovery Resources Press.
In this book, 88 couples talk about how they have coped with the problem of addictive sexual behavior.

Facing Heartbreak: Steps to Recovery for Partners of Sex Addicts by Carnes, S., Lee, M., & Rodrigues, R. Gentle Path Press
When you discover that the person you loved and trusted most in the world is hiding a secret life as a sex addict, the result can be devastating. Facing that heartbreak is what this book is all about. The healing process will take time regardless of whether you decide to stay in the relationship or leave. (From the online description.)

Cybersex Exposed: Simple Fantasy or Obsession? By Schneider, J. & Weiss, R. (2001) Center City, MN: Hazelden Publishing & Educational Services.
The authors examine the negative consequences of Internet sex addiction on health, career, intimacy and family relationships.

Your Sexually Addicted Spouse: How Partners Can Cope and Heal by Steffens, B. (2009). Far Hills, NJ: New Horizon Press.
Steffens' research shows that partners are not codependents but post-traumatic stress victims, while Marsha Means' provides insights, strategies, and critical steps to recognize, deal with, and heal partners of sexually addicted relationships.

Steps to Freedom (2nd ed.). by Weiss, D. (2000). Colorado Springs, CO: Discovery Press. The Twelve-steps are followed from a Christian perspective. It breaks down the various principles to help the reader experience freedom from sex addiction.

Cruise Control: Understanding Sex Addiction in Gay Men by Weiss R. (2011).

Leads men to a better understanding of the difference between sexual compulsion and non-addictive sexual behavior within the gay experience, and it explains what resources are available for recovery.

Appendix C

Counseling and Support Programs

Where can help be found?

Help for the sexually addicted comes in many forms. The Appendix provides venues for counseling and Twelve Step programs.

Individual counseling

Society for the Advancement of Sexual Health (SASH) provides a Web site where the names of sex addiction counselors are published for specific locations.

The Web site is http://wwwsashnet/

When the words sexual addiction counseling is entered a search engine, many hits are returned. Modify your search to sex addiction counselor followed by your city and state.

Twelve-step programs

The following is an inventory of the major Twelve Step and related programs that are available to those who are seeking recovery from sexual addiction. This author endorses Twelve Step programs but does not endorse a specific Twelve Step program.

Twelve-step programs for the partner or significant other Codependents of Sexual Addiction (COSA)

The Web site is http://wwwcosa-recoveryorg/

Codependents of Sexual Addiction (COSA) is a recovery program for men and women whose lives have been affected by compulsive sexual behavior.

S-Anon Family Groups
The Web site is http://wwwsanonorg/

S-Anon programs are for the fellowship of relatives and friends of sex-addicted people who share their experience, strength, and hope to solve their common problems.

Twelve-step programs for the addict

Christians in Recovery
The Web site is http://christians-in-recoveryorg/wp/

Christians in recovery (CIR) is a recovery program dedicated to mutual sharing of faith, strength, and hope as we live each day in recovery.

Sex Addicts Anonymous (SAA)
The Web site is http://wwwsexaaorg/

Sex Addicts Anonymous (SAA) is a fellowship of men and women who share their experiences, strength, and hope so they may overcome their sexual addiction and help others recover from sexual addiction and dependency.

Sexual Compulsives Anonymous (SCA)
The Web site is http://wwwsca-recoveryorg/

Sexual Compulsives Anonymous (SCA) is a Twelve Step fellowship of men and women who share their experience, strength and hope with each other, so that they may solve their common problem and help others to recover from sexual compulsion.

Sex and Love Addicts Anonymous (SLAA)
The Web site is http://wwwslaafwsorg/

Sex and love Addicts Anonymous (SLAA) is a Twelve Step Tradition oriented fellowship. Members seek a relationship with a higher power to counter the destructive consequences of one or more addictive behaviors related to sex addiction, love addiction, dependency or romantic attachments, emotional dependency, and sexual, social and emotional anorexia.

Sexual Recovery Anonymous (SRA)
The Web site is http://wwwsexualrecoveryorg/

Sexual Recovery Anonymous (SRA) is a fellowship of men and women who share their experience, strength, and hope with each other that they may solve their common problem and help others to recover. Their primary purpose is to stay sexually sober and help others achieve sobriety.

Meet Mary Lou (Warren) Swanberg, Author, Coach and Counselor

I thank all who will cherish this book and pray for your recovery and/or your mission to assist someone you love with theirs. During my life I have been blessed by many careers and opportunities which led me to where I can share the skills and wisdom I have learned along my journey.

My career covers multiple industries, beginning in New York City in fashion design. Subsequently, I spent 30+ years in the Communication industry working in trade shows, television, advertising, direct marketing, professional calligraphy, and founding a 20 person graphic communications firm.

With the help of my son, I entered the homeschooling arena where I applied my communication skills by hosting homeschooling conferences around the US. In addition, I was a veteran columnist for an online magazine and an on-air consultant during which time I appeared on global, national and regional TV and radio.

Concurrently with these wonderful career experiences, I was surrounded by trauma and addiction from multiple sources. Always a student interested in human behavior, I was privileged to work with Kids Watch and Family Resources, two organizations that build resiliency in children at risk for gang activity and that offered sexual abuse treatment to individuals, families and offenders, respectively. Recently, I have become a Certified High Performance Coach from High Performance Institute and a Certified Trainer for Power Braining ™. My goal is to help re-create and heal lives that have been damaged by abuse -- be it substance, emotional or physical.

Currently, I work with my beloved husband, George as a counselor and life coach at our practice, Lifeline Counseling 4 Addictions in Northern Virginia. It is through this work that we have become involved in mental health issues and human trafficking since there is cross-over with substance abuse and addiction.

I draw strength from my Faith. I believe that Jesus Christ is Love and Healing and came to redeem every person regardless of the life they have lived. I will imitate the life-giving love of Christ in all aspects of my life

May this book bring you understanding, hope, and sobriety. I welcome your feedback and can be reached at marylouswanberg@gmail.com

About the Author

Meet Paul Becker, Author

Counseling and writing are second careers. I served as a Federal Civil Servant for over 36 years. Working with men in prison led me back to school where I earned a master's degree in counseling education. I am in a private practice in Fairfax City, Virginia.

Before I became a counselor, I was employed by the U. S. Department of Labor. I began my Federal career as a Labor Economist, served as the Chief Financial Officer for The Bureau of Labor Statistics, and as a senior manager in the Office of the Secretary of Labor. I have multiple advanced degrees from St. Francis University, Harvard University, JFK School of Government, and The Virginia Polytechnic Institute and State University. I earned my LPC license in 2002.

For the last 16 years I served as a sex addiction therapist at the Lifeline Counseling Center in Fairfax City. I have written twelve books on the subject. (See the next page for a list of my books available through Amazon.com).

The third edition of *Recovery from Sexual Addiction: A Path to Recovery* includes over 100 pages of additional content than the second edition. Edition two, *Recovery from Sexual Addiction: A Man's Guide* is available as a talking book from Amazon.com as will the third edition in mid-2019. The recovery series address men who contemplate recovery but are looking for answers to many questions. In particular they ask why they are engrossed in aberrant sexual behavior and what would their life be like if they gave up their long life friend...sexual addiction.

A companion edition, *What a Woman Needs to Know about Male Sexual Addiction*, is available for women seeking to understand why their partners are sexually addicted and to help women decide their future. It is a second edition, and a third edition is now available

I enjoy our connection through my books and offer you the opportunity to provide feedback: Pbecker11@hotmail.com

Books Authored by Paul Becker, LPC

Letters from Paul

In Search of Recovery: A Christian Man's Guide (1st Ed)

In Search of Recovery Workbook: A Christian Man's Guide (1st Ed)

In Search of Recovery: Clinical Guide

Why Is My Partner Sexually Addicted? Insight women Need (1st Ed)

Recovery from Sexual Addiction: A Man's Guide (2nd Ed.)

Recovery from Sexual Addiction: A Man's Workbook (2nd Ed.)

Clinical Guide for the Treatment of Male Sexual Addiction

Sexual Addiction: Understanding and Treatment:
Textbook and Reference Manual

What a Woman Needs to Know about Sexual Addiction (2nd Ed.)

What a Woman Needs to Know about Sexual Addiction (3nd Ed.)

The WHY Book

The FREEDOM Book from Sexual Addiction (Currently not in print)

Recovery from Sexual Addiction: A Path to Sexual Recovery (3rd Ed.)

To contact Paul Becker and or to purchase a book, my e-mail is:
Pbecker11@hotmail.com
Books can also be purchased on Amazon.com (or many other vendors).
Enter Paul Becker, LPC into the Amazon browser.

Made in the USA
Middletown, DE
20 June 2023

33052723R00117